Butler's Rangers

Chas. M. Lefferts

Butler's Rangers

Three Accounts of the
American War of Independence

The Story of Butler's Rangers and
the Settlement of Niagara
Ernest Cruikshank

The Story of Cherry Valley
Henry U. Swinnerton

Wyoming Valley a Sketch of
Its Early Annals
Isaac A. Chapman

LEONAUR

Butler's Rangers
Three Accounts of the American War of Independence
The Story of Butler's Rangers and the Settlement of Niagara
by Ernest Cruikshank
The Story of Cherry Valley by Henry U. Swinnerton
Wyoming Valley a Sketch of Its Early Annals by Isaac A. Chapman

First published under the titles
The Story of Butler's Rangers and the Settlement of Niagara,
The Story of Cherry Valley
and
Wyoming Valley a Sketch of Its Early Annals
taken from Isaac A. Chapman's History of Wyoming.

Leonaur is an imprint of Oakpast Ltd

Copyright in this form © 2011 Oakpast Ltd

ISBN: 978-0-85706-711-1(hardcover)
ISBN: 978-0-85706-712-8 (softcover)

http://www.leonaur.com

Publisher's Notes

The opinions of the authors represent a view of events in which he
was a participant related from his own perspective,
as such the text is relevant as an historical document.

The views expressed in this book are not necessarily
those of the publisher.

Contents

The Story of Butler's Rangers and the Settlement of Niagara

Ernest Cruikshank

Contents

Preface

Many thousand descendants of the brave men who formed Butler's Rangers are now living in Ontario and other British Provinces. I hold that they have no reason to be ashamed of ancestors who were eminently distinguished by the none too common virtues of inalterable loyalty, unfailing courage, and unconquerable endurance, and who sacrificed everything for the cause which they had embraced. To them, at least, I feel that no apology is necessary in presenting a narrative which will not be found unduly eulogistic. It has been my aim to make a fair statement of the facts by sifting the evidence on both sides. It may be said that these were hard, fierce, and revengeful men, but it should be remembered that they lived in a stormy time, in a hard, fierce, and revengeful world. Their story has never yet been told from a sympathetic, or even a fair-minded, point of view.

The present narrative is based chiefly upon unpublished official documents, but every book and pamphlet bearing in any way upon the subject, within the writer's reach, has also been consulted.

Fort Erie, 27th February, 1893.

The Story of Butler's Rangers and the Settlement of Niagara

In the year 1774, the Province of New York, although probably the wealthiest and undoubtedly the most flourishing of the British Colonies in America, did not contain a free population much exceeding a quarter of a million. Of these, 39,000 were freeholders, entitled to vote at elections. The settlements were clustered along the banks of the Hudson, and extended up to the valley of the Mohawk nearly to its source, but nowhere did they run very far back from those rivers or some tributary stream, such as the Schoharie or Cobus Kill, which offered an easy means of communication with the outer world at all seasons. A few old Dutch families still possessed those enormous estates which they had acquired before the English conquest, and stubbornly refused to part with them at any price, or even to lease except on the most arbitrary of terms. Their conduct more than any other cause had tended to delay the settlement of the Province.

Outside of New York itself, Albany, having a population of about 5,000, was the largest and busiest town. Since the conquest of Canada it had become the seat of much of the fur trade with the Indians, and bade fair to eclipse Montreal. The merchants or their agents engaged in this traffic usually spent the summer at Oswego, where they met the Indians from the north and west, and the Mohawk River became the great highway for their goods. The greed and unscrupulousness of the Albany trader had become proverbial throughout the colonies. By the people of New England they were cordially hated, for during the late French wars they had not only sold the hostile Indians arms and ammunition, but had taken in exchange the spoils of ravaged New England villages, such as silver plate with the names of the owners still engraved on it, and, it was said, had encouraged them to get more. In their fury the New Englanders had even threatened to burn Albany at the first opportunity, and its inhabitants returned their hate with interest.

The valleys of the Mohawk and its principal tributary from the south, the Schoharie Kill, were frequently termed the "Garden of the Province," being composed of rich deep virgin soil, easy of cultivation, and yielding enormous crops of grass and grain. Stretching for some fifty miles along either bank of the Upper Mohawk, but nowhere more than two miles in width, lay a noted fertile tract, called, from the nationality of its inhabitants, the German Hats. The neighbouring hillsides were clothed with majestic pines, and the hum of the saw mill was heard on every petty creek. A numerous fleet of small sailing vessels was constantly employed in carrying the varied products of this region to the sea coast. So marked was the general prosperity of the province, during the twenty years preceding the revolution, that a regretful Loyalist has termed this period the "Garden Age of New York."

By far the best known and most influential man in the Province was Sir William Johnson, superintendent of the Northern Indians. For thirty years he had performed the duties of his difficult office with consummate skill and unvarying success. His influence over the Indians has never been equalled by any other white man, but to secure it he found himself obliged to conform to their habits in many discreditable ways, and even to blink at their vices and crimes. At times he wore their costume, painted his face and joined them in the war-dance. During the French war he had induced the Colonial Legislature to pay them a reward for scalps. Hundreds of them frequently were entertained by him alone at his storehouse at Castle Johnson, with perfect confidence and fearlessness in the midst of quantities of everything most coveted by them.

An acquaintance said that he united in his mode of life "the calm urbanity of a liberal and extensive trader with the splendid hospitality, the numerous attendance and the plain, though dignified, manners of an ancient baron." Although he did not by any means neglect his private interests in his relations with the Indians, and obtained large tracts of land from them for the merest trifle, this was done in such a direct and straightforward way that they took no offence, and he jealously protected them from the exactions and fraudulent schemes of others. Yet, whenever Indians attempted to over-reach him, they seldom failed to get the worst of it. In early life a Mohawk chief one day informed him at a council that he had dreamed the night before that Johnson had given him a handsome laced coat, which he thought was the same one he then had on.

Knowing their superstitious reverence for dreams. Sir William looked at him sharply and inquired whether he had really dreamed this, and, upon being assured that he had, took off the coat without hesitation and presented it to him. Next morning his turn came, and he remarked to the Indians that, although not in the habit of dreaming, he had dreamed a very curious dream during the night. On being urged to tell it he said he had dreamed that they had given him a large tract f land, extending for nine miles along the Mohawk River, to build a house on and form a settlement. The chief at once said, with apparent cheerfulness, that if the white man had actually dreamed that he must have the land, but he added, ruefully, that he would never dream with him again.

At the end of the last French war the King had granted Johnson a tract of land containing a hundred thousand aces, at a pepper corn rent, as a reward for his great services. This was known as the Royal Grant, and upon it, in 1764, he built a spacious mansion near the Cayadutta River, and during the three following years he created the thriving village of Johnstown, whither he attracted several merchants, a physician, and mechanics of every kind. There he built a stone church and a large inn, which was conducted by Captain Gilbert Tice, a veteran of the French wars. No travellers of note, however, were permitted to remain over night at this tavern, but were absolutely forced to accept the hospitality of the owner of the hall. Consequently, besides his own numerous family, Sir William had seldom less than ten and sometimes as many as thirty guests. Frequently eight or ten of the latter were Indian chiefs from distant parts of the continent. To supply the ordinary wants of his own household alone, twenty-four oxen and a hundred hogs were slaughtered annually. His superb and prodigal hospitality made him well-known to hundreds who otherwise would have scarcely heard his name.

His early marriage with Catharine Weissenberg had made him popular among the German settlers. For some time after her death he lived loosely, and had several illegitimate children. During the last twenty years of his life he cohabited with Mary Brant, a Mohawk woman of agreeable manners and unusual ability, whom he styled his housekeeper, but who was regarded by her own tribe as his lawful wife. They lived together with every appearance of union and affection. She gained much influence over him, for her adroitness and knowledge of their languages proved extremely useful to him in his dealings with the Indians. Aside from his official duties, his activity in public affairs was conspicuous in many ways.

Many poor immigrants were assisted by him to obtain lands. He imported blood horses and improved breeds of sheep for the benefit of the community. Churches were built in every important settlement for the use of Calvinist or Lutheran alike, without distinction, at his sole expense, and he aided liberally in the foundation of schools for both whites and Indians. When he succeeded in having an immense territory, extending from the outskirts of Schenectady to the Indian frontier, and from the Mohawk branch of the Deleware northward to the St. Lawrence, set apart under the name of Tryon County, in honour of the last British governor of the province, Johnson at once built a stone court house and gaol at Johnstown, which he presented to the people.

The last ten years of his life were occupied by a ceaseless struggle to maintain peace between the whites and the Indians under his charge, and to protect the latter against the encroachments and swindling plots of the unscrupulous traders and land-jobbers that swarmed on the frontiers of every province. With a set purpose he encouraged the intermarriage of the races. As already mentioned, he had already given a not very creditable example by living with an Indian woman. On one occasion, in 1768, he was present at the marriage of eighteen young white women with as many Indian chiefs.

He became a favourite mediator and referee in disputes arising among the Indians themselves, and more than once negotiated treaties of peace between the Six Nations and western or southern tribes. The Iroquois Confederacy rewarded his services by the gift of the "Salt Lake Onondaga," and all the land surrounding it for two miles in depth.

Usually a silent man, he became fluent and even eloquent on a fitting occasion. Like the Indians, he possessed a marvellous command of temper and perfect control of his countenance under the most trying circumstances. These points of similarity with them may have assisted him to acquire and retain his influence, but it cannot be denied that his treatment of them was marked by unvarying and inflexible honesty and justice.

Sir William Johnson died in a sudden and startling manner while engaged in holding a general council with the Indians at Johnson

Hall, in July, 1774. The day was extremely hot, and the Indians were much exasperated by the recent murder of several of their people by the whites, and other wrongs. After delivering a long and persuasive address, with all his old-time vigour. Sir William retired to his private room, where he sat down and drank a glass of wine. He then leaned back in the chair and expired without a groan. His death at such a critical time, when the Indians were discontented and the first mutterings of the coming storm were beginning to be heard throughout the province, was a staggering blow to the Loyalists of New York, and left a gap in their ranks that none could fill.

Had he lived there is good reason to believe that the whole population of the Mohawk valley would have risen in arms at his command, and that he would have exerted himself in defence of the "Unity of the Empire" with all his former tact and energy. Much of his work was soon undone by the devastating hand of war, his family and friends were driven into exile to renew the struggle in a distant wilderness, yet there was no impropriety in ranking him among the "Makers of America," although, perhaps, not in the restricted sense in which that term has been lately used.

His son, Sir John Johnson, then thirty-two years of age, was a comparative stranger to the people, having lived much in Albany and New York both before and after his marriage with Miss Watts, an heiress and lady of fashion. Naturally reserved and distant in his manners, he was far less popular than his father. Yet, such was the family influence, that he had been easily elected a member of the Assembly a few years before over Philip Schuyler, the candidate of the Livingston party, an active and energetic politician who had gained great wealth as an army contractor, and was not over scrupulous in his methods. At the time of his death. Sir William Johnson, next to the Penn family, was the greatest land holder in British America.

Sir John inherited Johnson Hall and the large surrounding estate, the lands surrounding Onondaga lake, besides most of his father's personal property. His sisters, one of whom had married her cousin, Guy Johnson of Guy Park, the other, Colonel Daniel Claus, each received fourteen thousand acres. Sir William's housekeeper. Miss Molly, as she was usually styled, was liberally provided for, and to each of her six children he bequeathed £1,500 and 3,000 acres, and a like quantity of land to each of her four sisters and two brothers, and to Joseph Brant and his brother.

His sons-in-law had acted as his deputies in the management of

17

Indian affairs for a dozen years, Guy Johnson in the capacity of superintendent of the Six Nations and Western Indians and Claus in the same relation to the Canadian tribes, and each had received a careful training in their duties: but it soon became manifest that both were woefully deficient in the requisite tact and energy, to say nothing of graver faults. Some time before his death he had formally recommended Guy Johnson as his successor in office.

Next to these two men in rank and local influence, but far surpassing both in natural ability, courage, and experience, stood John Butler. Sixty-five years before, his father, a young Irish subaltern, claiming descent from the illustrious family of Ormonde, had come to America with his regiment, from which he exchanged into one of the independent companies formed for service in the colonies, and afterwards incorporated as the Royal Americans or 60th. He held some important commands on the frontier, and acquired considerable influence among the Indians, although he never gained promotion. In the course of his service he made himself useful to Sir William Johnson, who in return exerted himself for the advancement of Butler's family. By the purchase of land from the Indians, the elder Butler secured a large and valuable property. One tract lying about seven miles from Johnstown, containing sixty thousand acres, was long known as Butler's purchase. He died in 1760, at the age of ninety, having been a lieutenant in the British army for seventy years.

John Butler, his eldest son, was born at New London, Conn., in 1725, and educated in the same province. In allusion to this circumstance Colonel Claus, by whom he was heartily disliked, accused him of flattery and cunning, "having been born and bred in New England." When Sir William Johnson received command of the expedition against Crown Point in 1755, he nominated John Butler and his brother Walter as captains in the Indian department. In the disastrous battle of the 8th September of that year, Walter Butler, Farrel Wade, Johnson's own brother-in-law, and the celebrated Mohawk Chief, Hendrick, were killed, but John Butler distinguished himself greatly and escaped unhurt.

He served under Abercromby at Ticonderoga and with Bradstreet at the capture of Fort Frontenac. He then accompanied Johnson against Fort Niagara as second in command of the Indians, and succeeded him in the entire charge of them after General Prideaux's death. In that station he shared in the victory over the relieving force which so signally avenged Braddock's defeat, and it was said acted

18

with "spirit, bravery, and resolution, and was foremost in pursuit of the enemy." After the surrender of the garrison, he was appointed a member of the court established there for the trial of civil cases. In 1760 he went with General Amherst to Montreal as second in command of the Indians. During Pontiac's war, he was actively and successfully employed in the difficult task of restraining the Six Nations from joining the hostile Indians.

Owing to his intimate knowledge of several Indian languages, he was constantly employed by Sir William Johnson up to the hour of his death as interpreter at the most important councils. He then resided on his fine estate of Butlersburg, near Caughnawaga, and was one of the Judges of the County Court and Lieutenant-Colonel of Guy Johnson's regiment of militia. Sir William Johnson had nominated him an executor of his will, but from some unknown cause he had incurred the pronounced dislike, if not the positive enmity, not only of Sir John Johnson but of both his brothers-in-law, who were intimately associated with Butler in his civil and military functions. Fearing that he would be dismissed in consequence, the Indians petitioned that, he might continue to act as their interpreter and Guy Johnson was constrained to give his consent. Besides his wife, his family consisted of Walter, the eldest son, lately admitted to the bar, "a youth of spirit, sense, and ability;" Thomas, still under twenty, two younger sons, and a daughter.

The power of the Loyalist party was probably greater in New York than in any other province, but their leaders lacked the courage and decision of character needful to turn it to the best advantage. The wealthy merchants, the proprietors of the great feudal manors, the adherents of the Church of England, more numerous here than elsewhere, the Dutch farmers, and the recent German immigrants, were generally disposed to be loyal or absolutely neutral. In the City of New York, two-thirds of all the property was owned by Loyalists, and outside there was scarcely a symptom of disaffection. But there was a small party of violent revolutionists prepared to go any length, and they dangled before the eyes of many discontented, lawless men almost irresistible temptations to join them. There was an enormous quantity of land held by a few active loyalists which might be parcelled out among their followers; there was, too, a debt of eight or nine millions of pounds due to British merchants which might be repudiated. There was, besides, illimitable liberty to gratify their passions and do whatever seemed right in their own eyes.

In January, 1775, a motion in the New York Assembly to consider the proceeding of the Continental Congress was lost by a vote of eleven to ten. Soon, after, a vote of thanks to the delegates from the province was proposed and negatived, fifteen to nine, and a resolution for the appointment of new delegates to the next Congress was rejected by seventeen to nine. The last Provincial Assembly had therefore strongly indicated its disapproval of the acts of the Congress, and refused to share the responsibility for them. The inhabitants of Tryon County were, to all appearance, among the most loyal and contented. Their representatives, Guy Johnson and Hendrick Frey, had never swerved from their allegiance. Governor Tryon visited the valley in 1772, and wrote rapturously of the evident prosperity and contentment of the people, "who were not less seemingly pleased with the presence of their Governor than he with them."

He reviewed the militia and reported that it exceeded 1,400 men under arms. The great proprietors and wealthy families here were Loyalists to a man. Besides the members of the Johnson family, the Bradts, Freys, Hares, Herkimers, Thompsons and Youngs, John Butler, Joseph Chew, John Dease, Robert Lottridge, Hendrick Nelles, Peter Ten Broeck, Alexander White, and many others, imperilled handsome estates, which in the end were confiscated. Large tracts of land were owned by absentee Loyalists, such as the Cosbys, DeLanceys, DePeysters, Waltons, and Tryon himself, and these eventually shared the same fate.

Already in June, 1774, the supervisors of that county had flatly refused to take sides in the dispute with Great Britain, declaring their opinion "that it did not appear to tend to the violation of their civil or religious rights, but merely regarded a single article of commerce which no person was compelled to purchase, and which persons of real virtue and resolution might easily have avoided or dispensed with." At the quarter sessions held in the following March, the judges, sheriff, clerk, magistrates and grand jury reaffirmed these sentiments, adding that they "abhorred, and do still abhor, all measures tending through partial representation to alienate the affections of the subjects from the Crown, or by wresting the interest and meaning of a particular act to draw in the inhabitants of a wide and extensive territory to a dangerous and rebellious opposition to the parent state, when exerting itself to preserve that obedience without which no state can exist. They do therefore resolve to bear faithful and true allegiance to their lawful sovereign. King George the Third, and that in the true and plain sense of the words, as they are, or ought to be, commonly understood without prevarication, which has often accompanied the same expressions from his warmest opponents."

No organized revolutionary movement made its appearance in the county until May, 1775, when it seems to have been suppressed by force. A Whig committee was next formed at Cherry Valley, but its members were evidently conscious that as yet they represented an uninfluential and insignificant local minority. On the 18th of May they complained to the Committee of Safety in Albany that "this county has for a series of years been ruled by one family, the several branches of which are still strenuous in dissuading the people from coming into Congressional measures, and have even last week, at a numerous meeting of the Mohawk district, appeared with all their dependents armed to oppose the people considering of their grievances: their number being so great, and the people unarmed, they struck terror into most of them and they dispersed."

Guy Johnson afterwards scornfully described this meeting as having been called by an "itinerant New England leather-dresser, and conducted by others, if possible more contemptible. I had therefore little inclination to revisit such men, or attend to their absurdities." A "liberty pole," erected at this time or very soon afterwards, was cut down by the sheriff

Despite this check, the spirit of discontent continued to make headway. Sir William Johnson's latest project for improving his estates and peopling the country, which was being vigorously carried out by his son, filled the minds of many of the original settlers with vague suspicion and alarm. For the most part they were descendants of sturdy Palatine recusants that had suffered the extremity of ill for conscience sake, and to whom the very name of Papist was abominable. For once Johnson failed to fathom the intensity of their religious prejudice. Though born in Ireland and bearing an Anglicised name, he traced his descent in the direct line from the MacIan branch of the McDonnels of Glencoe.

A feeling of kinship prompted him to enter into a correspondence which led to the immigration in 1773 of the McDonnels of Aberchallader, Collachie, Leek, and Scottus in Glengarry, with many of their relatives and dependents, forming a body of more than six hundred persons. They were all Roman Catholics. A few of the leaders purchased lands; the remainder were established as tenants on the Johnson estates, and were supplied by Sir John with food, cattle, and agricultural implements, valued by him at £2,000 during the next two years. To the peaceful German farmers around them they seemed a rude, fierce, and quarrelsome race, constantly wearing dirk and broad sword, and much given over to superstition and idolatrous practices.

Accordingly, when the local Whig Committee announced that Sir John Johnson had fortified the hall and surrounded himself with a body of Highland Roman Catholics for its defence, they could not have appealed to the inhabitants in a more effective way. They had already learned to dislike the Highlanders, and they detested their religion. The Johnsons and their friends, however, made no further effort to meet their opponents, but stood strictly on the defensive. Elsewhere throughout the Province the Loyalists, though numerous, were hesitating and timid, the Revolutionary party daring and aggressive. Accordingly, they were constrained to negotiate and temporize.

To the westward lay the country of the Six Nations. The boundary separating their territory from Tryon County followed the Oswego River, Oneida Lake, and the Tienaderha branch of the Susquehanna. They often termed their confederacy, "the Long House," of which the Senecas residing on the Susquehanna and Ohio guarded the western, and the Mohawks the eastern, door, while the Onondagas kept the council fire in the centre. By the ravages of pestilence and almost incessant warfare their numbers had gradually dwindled to less than ten thousand, of whom about one-fifth were warriors. The Mohawks, although still regarded as the bravest and most influential, was the least numerous of all the tribes. They occupied three small straggling villages, two on the Mohawk and one in the vale of Schoharie, which were quite surrounded on all sides by populous white settlements.

They numbered less than five hundred persons, nearly the whole of whom professed Christianity under the instruction of the Church of England missionary, Mr. Stuart. Just outside the boundary, near the borders of Oneida Lake, lived the Oneidas in two villages called old and new Oneida. They could turn out 250 warriors. Six miles beyond these lay the Tuscarora village, inhabited by a hundred men capable of bearing arms. The Onondagas, residing near the lake which still bears their name, could muster 150 warriors. A considerable number of these three tribes, which were closely connected by frequent intermarriages, had been nominally converted by Presbyterian missionaries from New England.

The Cayugas, numbering two hundred fighting men, lived chiefly in one large village near Lake Cayuga. A chain of Seneca villages extended from within fifty miles of Cayuga Lake to the upper waters of the Ohio, and were roughly estimated to contain a thousand warriors. On the eastern branch of the Susquehanna the remnant of four allied or vassal tribes from the southward had settled not long before, on lands allotted to them by the Six Nations. Three western tribes were likewise united with them in close alliance, and regarded them as their "elder brothers." These were the Delewares (600) inhabiting the Susquehanna and Muskingum, the Shawanese, (300) on the Scioto, and the Hurons (200) on the Sandusky.

As a whole the Six Nations had made considerable advances in civilization.

> Were they savages, (said Mrs. Grant of Laggan, writing from personal observation), who had fixed habitations; who cultivated rich fields; who built castles (for so they called their not incommodious wooden houses, surrounded with palisades); who planted maize and beans, and showed considerable ingenuity in constructing and adorning their canoes, arms, and clothing? They who had wise though unwritten laws and conducted their wars, treaties, and alliances with deep and sound policy; they whose eloquence was bold and nervous and animated; whose language was sonorous, musical, and expressive; who possessed generous and elevated sentiments, heroic fortitude and unstained probity?

The Mohawks, whose principal "castle" stood almost within the shadow of Johnson Hall, had lived for years in closest association with their white neighbours. Thirty years before, Sir William Johnson had been received into their tribe and his fondness for them was so marked that they were frequently described as his Indians. They had been often led into battle by Butler, Hare, Lottridge and other provincial officers. Many of them had white blood flowing in their veins. They had generally adopted the dress and many customs of the whites, and taken on at least a thin veneer of European civilization. Sir John Johnson they regarded as one of "their own blood," and they constantly professed the warmest attachment to the English, "Nothing less than manifest injury,"

Governor Tryon had remarked some years before;

> . . . .in my opinion will drive the Mohawks from their steady attachment to His Majesty's interest. They appear to be actuated

23

as a community by principles which would do honour to the most civilized nations. Indeed, they are in civilized state, and many of them good farmers

The Senecas and Cayugas, on the other hand, still rigidly adhered to their ancient rites and customs.

For some months past the Whigs of New England had been secretly endeavouring to enlist the Indians on their side in the coming struggle. Among the decadent tribes of Massachusetts and Connecticut their efforts had already been crowned with entire success, and several bands of these allies had aided them actively during the siege of Boston. In the missionaries Kirkland and Crosby, stationed among the Oneidas and Onondagas, they now found ready and ardent partisans. During the winter Guy Johnson learned that these "weak but furious zealots" were trying to engage these Indians in the civil war. They openly assured their congregations that "the King was set against the Americans and Indians," that they must expect no further attention from him as he had stopped all goods coming to America, and consequently gunpowder, so necessary to them in hunting, would soon cost three or four dollars a gill.

The faction that had opposed the missionaries complained to Johnson that they had refused to baptize their children, and denounced Crosby in particular as "a busy man interested in trade and things we always thought unbecoming to a clergyman." In reply the superintendent cautiously advised them that "they might signify their disgust in a manner that becomes moderate men towards a minister, whose person should always be treated with respect on account of his sacred profession." But in his letter to Lord Dartmouth he said;

> I see plainly, unless timely prevented, some extraordinary steps may be taken to embarrass the Government and its officers, the Indians being in a state of suspense rather than any other until their different disputes are accommodated.

In common with other tribes the Six Nations had many grave grounds for dissatisfaction. The Mohawks were resisting a most iniquitous conspiracy to evict them from the very lands on which their largest village was built. Their allies on the Susquehanna were alarmed and irritated when they learned that the boundary line, lately run from Owegy on that river to the Deleware, took from them four of their settlements, plainly contrary to the intention of the treaty of 1788. They had not forgotten that in the past large tracts of the richest lands upon those rivers had been wrested from them by fraud and forgery. At the same time the Shawanese were deeply exasperated by the unlawful irruption of a thousand armed settlers from Virginia upon their favourite hunting grounds in Kentucky, in open defiance of a solemn treaty, backed by royal proclamation.

To dispel the suspicions of the Indians and diminish expenses, the regular troops had been long since withdrawn from all forts on the borders of their territory except Oswegatchie, Niagara, Detroit, and Mackinac, and the garrisons of these posts were reduced to the lowest point, while their defences had been permitted to fall into ruins. This polity, in conjunction with the incessant efforts of the agents of the Crown to prevent intrusion on their lands, resulted only in embittering the inhabitants of the border against the British Government without conferring the slightest benefit upon the Indians. The back settlements had become, as usual, a refuge for the runaways, escaped convicts, and all the offscourings of colonial rascaldom. The advance guard of European civilization was undeniably disreputable. The lawless conduct of these men, and the story of their wanton aggressions upon the Indians, is vividly related in Sir William Johnson's voluminous correspondence.

> When we consider the encroachments made towards the Ohio, (he wrote to Lord Shelburne), the grievances complained of concerning unjust grants in other parts of the country yet unredressed, the robberies and murders committed on their people on the frontiers of the provinces to the southward yet unpunished, and the irregularity with which the trade is conducted through the want of sufficient powers to regulate it, it is not surprising that the Indians, who are the most suspicious people in the world, should be actuated by a spirit of strong resentment.

> The repeated acts of cruelty committed in the different provinces hitherto unpunished, the intrusions upon their lands and bad claims, together with the rest of their grievances, all of which are still unredressed, have operated so strongly on their suspicious minds.

> Their malevolence and disregard of all treaties is still demonstrated whenever they fall in the way of small parties or single Indians. When Indians are assembled on public affairs there are always traders secreted in the neighbourhood, and some pub-

licly, who not only make them intoxicated during the time intended for public business, but afterwards get back the greater part of their presents in exchange for spirituous liquors of the worst kind, thereby defeating the intentions of the Crown and causing them to commit many murders and disorders as well amongst the inhabitants as themselves.

They (the Indians) discover that the back inhabitants, particularly those who daily go over the mountains of Virginia, employ much of their time in hunting, interfering with them therein, have a hatred for, ill-treat, rob, and frequently murder the Indians; that they are in general a lawless set of people, as fond of independency as themselves, and more regardless of government, owing to ignorance, prejudice, democratical principle, and their remote situation. The Indians, likewise, perceive that our governments are weak and impotent, that whatever these people do their juries will acquit then, the landed men protect them, or a rabble rescue them from the hands of justice.

These settlers generally set out with a general prejudice against all Indians, and the young Indian warriors or hunters are too often inclined to retaliate. Most of these evils result from the rapid intrusion on their lands, and the unrestrained irregularities in trade to which I see no period.

In most of the Indian towns on our frontiers there are some idle fellows to be found who give themselves up entirely to case and drinking, and being cast out by the rest are made the instruments of the worst part of our people.

I have little hopes that settlements can be restrained by any ordinary measures where the multitude have for so many years discovered such an ungovernable passion for these lands and pay so little regard to a fair title or the authority of the American governments. So that with the artifices of designing men amongst them, the encroachments and many other acts of injustice of the inhabitants of most of the frontiers, the incapacity and (as it appears to the Indians) the unwillingness of our American Governments to redress them, the jealousy of the Indians is rather increased.

For more than ten years past the most dissolute fellows, united with debtors and persons of a wandering disposition, have been removing from Pennsylvania and Virginia, &c., into the Indian country towards the Ohio, and a considerable number of settlements were made as early as 1765, when my deputy was sent to the Illinois, from whence he gave me a particular account of the uneasiness it occasioned amongst the Indians. Many of these emigrants are idle fellows that are too lazy to cultivate lands, and invited by the plenty, of game they found have employed themselves in hunting, in which they interfere much more with the Indians than if they pursued agriculture alone, and the Indian hunters (who are composed of all the warriors in each nation) already begin to feel the scarcity this has occasioned, which greatly increases their resentment.

A few months before his death he referred "to the many murders committed by our people with impunity, of which there are no less than eighteen recent instances,"

The measure of wrong and injustice was filled to overflowing, and everything seemed ripe for a general rising of the Indians when Sir William Johnson's able hand was removed. Exasperated by a series of base and brutal murders in which Indian women and children were butchered without mercy, and scalped and mutilated by the frontiersmen of Virginia, the Shawanese broke from the control of Alexander McKee, Johnson's resident deputy, and began what is known as Cresap's or Lord Dunmore's war. The Six Nations were deeply stirred by their appeals for assistance, and a few of their younger warriors hastened to join them. In October, 1774, three hundred Shawanese, being the entire fighting force of the tribe, assisted by a few Mingos and others connected with them by marriage, were attacked by more than a thousand Virginian militia at the fork of the Great Kanawha River.

They resisted this very superior force for an entire day and adroitly made their escape across the river with trifling loss, after having killed and wounded nearly two hundred of their assailants. Meanwhile Guy Johnson and his deputies strove with desperate energy to restrain the Six Nations from joining in the conflict. In the end the chiefs agreed not only to recall the warriors that had already gone to the war, but to advise the Shawanese to make peace, which the latter then found themselves obliged to do. Before a treaty was concluded the startling information came from England that French agents had been sent to America to excite an Indian war, and the substantial truth of the warning was established by Colonel Butler, who succeeded in obtaining from the Senecas an "axe belt" presented to them by one *Sang-blanc*, a mysterious trader, with the significant message that "their French father was not dead, but sleeping." The Senecas confessed at the same time that there were other "bad belts" among the Shawanese.

Caravans of traders proceeding to the Indian country were waylaid and plundered by armed bands of white men, disguised as Indians in war paint and breech-clout.

To complete the prevailing anarchy of the borders, immigrants from Connecticut in the Wyoming Valley and from Virginia at Pittsburg had seized large tracts of land, and were holding them by force in defiance of the Provincial authorities of Pennsylvania. Small armies met in pitched battle, men were killed and dwellings burned in both places.

The trading posts and forts on the great lakes lay practically at the mercy of the Six Nations, as the garrisons were insufficient and the works had been permitted to decay until they were scarcely defensible. As long as the Indians continued friendly these posts would be tolerably secure, but if they became neutral or joined the enemy resistance against any attack would be hopeless. The capture of the forts would entail the loss of the North-western fur trade, upon which the commercial welfare of Canada then entirely depended. To preserve both, an alliance with the Indians was clearly indispensable Those who knew the Indians best on both sides agreed that it would be impossible to keep them neutral. To the educated Englishmen there can be little doubt their employment at first appeared much more objectionable than it did to the average colonist, who had been made familiar with it in former wars.

It is certain that Washington and Adams, Montgomery and Schuyler, and in fact the leaders of the revolution generally, approved of it with scarcely a symptom of hesitation, except on the ground of expense. Having already enlisted the Stockbridge Indians, the Congress of Massachusetts, on the 4th of April, 1775, sent a letter to the Missionary Kirkland at Oneida, requesting him to exert his influence with the Six Nations to induce them to join their forces, but if they refused to prevail upon them to remain neutral. An address to the Indians accompanied this letter. It was a marvel of ingenious misrepresentation.

Our fathers, (it said), were obliged by the cruelty of their brethren to leave their country, yet we have fought for them and conquered Canada and many other places which they have had and have not paid us for. They have refused to let us have powder and shot to send to the Indians. What would the Indians do without powder and shot? But we soon hope to supply them with both of our own making. They have made a law to establish the religion of the Pope in Canada.

Confidential agents were dispatched at the same time to solicit the assistance of the Indians of Canada and Nova Scotia. To each recruit from these tribes they promised a coat, blanket, and forty shillings a month. In these intrigues another New England clergy man, the Rev. Eleazar Wheelock of Dartmouth College, was very active. In May, Ethan Allen sent one Captain Ninham, a Stockbridge Indian, from Crown Point with a message to the Indians at Caughnawaga, in which he said:—

I want to have your warriors come and see me, and help me fight the King's regular troops. You know they stand all along close together, rank and file, and my men fight as Indians do, and I want your warriors to join me and my warriors like brothers and ambush the regulars; if you will, I will give you money, blankets, tomahawks, knives, paint, and anything there is in the army, just like brothers and I will go with you into the woods to scout, and my men and yours will sleep together, and eat and drink together, and fight regulars because they first killed our brothers and will fight against us; therefore, I want our brother Indians to help us fight, for I know Indians are good warriors and can fight well in the bush. You know it is good for my warriors und Indians too, to kill regulars, because they first began to kill our brothers in this country.

This letter was at once carried to General Carleton, who tried to counteract Allen's intrigues, although with small success at the time, as the influence of New England was strong among these Indians.

About the same time (14th May) Guy Johnson received simultaneous warnings from correspondents in Albany and Philadelphia that a plot had been formed to kidnap him. He assembled the officers of his department and a party of trusty men from his own regiment of militia, and fortified his house to resist an attack. A body of Mohawks gathered there to defend him, and without his knowledge, as he asserted, summoned the Oneidas to their assistance. Their message was intercepted and made use of to inflame the people against him. His movements were constantly watched by spies; letters passing to and from his house were opened and read; the supplies he had ordered for the use of the Indians were detained at Albany, and even trifling articles for his own household were withheld.

Threats of an attack were daily made; seditious toasts were drunk on public occasions, and persons were forced to sign articles of association against the government. Johnson reminded the committees that he had persuaded the Indians to remain quiet during the winter in the face of much provocation, and warned them that if they now found their supplies stopped, their council fire disturbed, and their superintendent insulted, they might yet take a dreadful revenge. His office was of the greatest importance to the safety of the frontiers and the interests of trade, and it was his duty to promote peace. "I desire," he said, "to enjoy liberty of conscience and the exercise of my own judgment, and that all others should have the same privilege."

The only instructions which Johnson had as yet received were contained in a letter from Lord Dartmouth, dated 1st February, 1775, in which the latter had remarked:

> The preserving the good will and affection of the Six Nations is an object of which we ought never to lose sight, and I hope through your zeal and endeavours we may avoid any ill consequences that may be expected to follow through the measures which may have been pursued by the Virginians.

His situation was daily growing more intolerable when he received a letter from General Gage, then besieged in Boston, and much enraged by his reverses. He announced that the besiegers had assembled every Indian they could engage, and that, in conjunction with their riflemen, these allies were continually firing on his sentries and outposts. In some of the skirmishes that had taken place, his wounded soldiers had been tomahawked and scalped. "In short," he concluded, "no time should be lost to distress a people so wantonly rebellious." Gage's letter decided Johnson's future course. He collected all the Mohawks that were at home, and being joined by about a hundred ardent loyalists, marched rapidly up the Mohawk towards the Indian frontiers.

Among those who accompanied were Daniel Claus, John and Walter Butler, Barent Frey, Hon Yost Herkimer, Gilbert Tice, Joseph Brant and at least two of Sir William Johnson's sons, besides many other men of weight and influence. As a whole his party was drawn from the flower of the population. His march caused great alarm among those who had reason to dread reprisals, and they raised the country in arms behind him under pretence of defending the frontier against the Indians, although they did not venture to oppose or attack him. Near the ruins of Fort Stanwix he met a large party of the Oneidas marching to his relief, but he was forced to leave them behind for want of provisions.

On the 17th of July he reached Oswego. A few days later he held a council there with 1450 Indians, including a deputation from the Hurons of Detroit. Cuyler, the mayor of Albany, who was following him up the Mohawk with several boats laden with provisions was detained by his enemies, and he was forced to send to Oswegatchie for supplies. He still professed the most peaceable intentions, but found little difficulty in persuading the Indians;

. . . . to resolve to co-operate with His Majesty's troops in defence of the communication and waters emptying into the St. Lawrence, and in the annoyance of the enemy, and to send their band of warriors present with him to Montreal to inspire their dependents there with the same resolution.

Means of transport were not available, and several weeks elapsed before he was able to set sail in a sloop and several *batteaux*, taking with him only 120 Indians. The flotilla arrived at Montreal in August, and Johnson advised the governor that it would be expedient to put the Indians in motion with as little delay as possible, as they could not endure being kept in idleness. Carleton replied that they must be amused in some other way, as he did not consider it wise to permit them to advance beyond the province line. In other words, he had determined to employ them on the defensive only. A few days later, 1600 Canadian Indians assembled there and agreed to adopt the same policy. Colonel Claus has recorded the arguments used by him to effect this result. He described;

. . . . the New Englanders insulting the troops and becoming the aggressors at Lexington; their unwarrantable and rebellious invasion of Canada, a country not the least concerned in the dispute; their being then in possession of the territory about Lake Champlain which His Majesty allotted to them for hunting and fishing; the danger of their losing those means of subsistence in case the rebels should get footing there. Their ill-usage of the Indians in general and stripping them of all their lands if not guarded against by the Crown; the striking example of their own people living among them, some of whom they made

31

slaves or servants of, and got their lands from them in a fraudulent manner, which would be the case with all the Indians should they become the rulers of the continent of America.

Six hundred warriors next attended a conference with the governor and openly proposed to warn the New Englanders to evacuate Ticonderoga and Crown Point, and in the event of a refusal to lay waste their frontiers. Carleton thanked them for their good will, but declared that all he wanted them to do was to station a party of their young men at St. Johns, to serve as scouts for that garrison and watch the movements of the enemy.

Fifty warriors were selected and sent forward under Captain Gilbert Tice, with Walter Butler and Peter Johnson (a natural son of Sir William) as his lieutenants. Their number was afterwards increased to 125, and on the 6th of September ninety of them ambushed and repelled with heavy loss a large body of Americans advancing to besiege that place. In this skirmish Captain Tice was badly wounded and Captain Daniel, "a faithful Mohawk," and several other Indians, were killed. On the 25th of September, Ethan Allen[1] appeared suddenly on the island of Montreal at the head of 140 men and advanced rapidly against the town, which was then quite unfortified and weakly garrisoned. Captain Crawford sallied out to meet the invaders with forty men of the 26th Regiment and a few volunteers from among the residents. He held them in check until Lieutenants Butler and Johnson, with thirty Rangers and Indians, briskly assailed them in the flank. The Americans took shelter in a large barn, but when a field-piece was brought against the building they surrendered at discretion. Lieut. Johnson, "an intrepid and active young man," took their leader with his own hand in the pursuit.

A few days later Guy Johnson once more requested permission to lead a body of Indians against the enemy, but was again refused, so reluctant was the governor to employ them in offensive operations. On learning his decision most of them returned home much discontented. Johnson and Claus at once applied for leave of absence, and sailed for England in November. Their conduct naturally appeared to Carleton very like a desertion of their post at a most trying and critical time, and finding that he himself would be inevitably shut up within the walls of Quebec during the winter, he despatched to Niagara Colonel Butler, who was next to them in rank in the department, and

1. Ethan Allen at Ticonderoga During the American War of Independence by Ethan Allen also published by Leonaur.

had been named by Johnson as his deputy during his absence.

Butler's instructions from the governor merely directed him to preserve the good will of the Indians and retain them in an attitude of absolute neutrality. This alone proved a task of supreme difficulty, as the country of the Six Nations was already overrun with spies and emissaries in the service of the Congress, of whom the missionaries Crosby and Kirkland, and the interpreter, Deane, were the most zealous and influential. They had even begun to plan the capture of Niagara, where there was a sufficient quantity of military stores to tempt an attack. The confidence of the Indians was greatly shaken by the successful invasion of Canada, which was continually being trumpeted in their ears by these men.

Butler summoned meeting after meeting with fluctuating success. He distributed presents with a liberal hand, and reminded the Indians alike of their recent pledges and their ancient friendship and alliance with the King. There is conclusive evidence that he faithfully obeyed his instructions and "spoke to them of nothing but peace," until March, 1776, when he received a message requiring him to send down a body of warriors to assist in the reconquest of the province. In this task he was quite successful. A hundred of the Senecas and Cayugas readily consented to go to Montreal to open a passage for traders and to "make a path," for Col. Johnson, whom they expected to return at that time.

At Oswegatchie they were joined by an equal number of Missassaugas, assembled from the north shore of Lake Ontario, and a small party of the 8th regiment, under Capt. Forster. The advanced post of the Americans at the Cedars, occupied by 400 men with two field-guns, surrendered to them after a very faint show of resistance, and a reinforcement of 120 more was cut to pieces next day. This sudden diversion contributed materially to force the enemy out of Montreal, and Butler felt, not unreasonably, that no small share of credit was due himself as the organizer of the expedition. In the meantime he had persuaded the Six Nations in a body to declare that they would take no part in the war, and to send a message to their western allies urging them to adopt the same policy.

Accordingly we find the western Indians informing the American agent at Pittsburg that they would not permit an army to pass through their country, and that consequently he must not think of attempting the expedition against Detroit, which had been talked of for some time past. Having thus for the moment secured the "Upper Posts" from all danger of an attack, Butler laboured steadily to strengthen his influence among the Indians. He knew that at every meeting spies in the pay of Congress had been present, who reported all that took place to their employers. In some instances these were white men, but usually they were Oneida or Deleware Indians, whom it was difficult to detect or exclude. His next step was to secure the expulsion of all known emissaries of the enemy from their territories.

Agents of his own were then quietly established in the principal villages to collect intelligence and keep the Indians in good humour. One of the ablest of these was William Caldwell, a young adventurer belonging to a good family in Philadelphia, who had assisted a number of British officers to escape from prison and safely guided them through the intervening wilderness to Niagara. Among others may be named Barent Frey, brother of Colonel Hendrick Frey of Tryon County, John Johnson, an Oneida trader of much experience, and William and Peter, half-blood sons of the late Sir William Johnson. A steady though slender tide of fugitives was already setting in from the border settlements, both of New York and Pennsylvania, to Niagara, and he was soon enabled to organize from them a body of thoroughly trustworthy and efficient assistants, most of whom were able to speak one or more Indian languages. Yet he failed to obtain the aid of Alexander McKee of Pittsburg, who was almost omnipotent among the Shawanese and other western tribes, for his letters were intercepted and McKee was instantly confined.

Despairing of success by any other means, the Americans began to concoct schemes for kidnapping Butler. At the general council of the confederacy Sangerachta, principal war-chief of the Senecas, publicly accused the Oneidas of having entertained such a proposal, and asserted that General Schuyler had promised them $250 for Butler's scalp or person. Rumour said the reward was subsequently increased to $1000. Schuyler's correspondence shows that the plan was approved, but there is no mention of the reward. The minds of most of the Indians continued unsettled and wavering to the end of the year. It was generally supposed that they would ultimately join the party they believed most likely to succeed, and it was admitted that it would be almost impossible to keep them neutral much longer. British victories in Canada in the early part of the year were nearly counterbalanced by the loss of Boston.

Intelligence of the capture of New York by General Howe and his subsequent successes, produced a remarkable sensation among them, and some tribes were with difficulty restrained from rising at once and attacking the frontiers. It was at this critical moment that Joseph Brant appeared among the Senecas, accompanied by Capt. Tice, bearing a verbal message from Guy Johnson to the Six Nations, desiring them to hold themselves in readiness to co-operate with Howe. They had made their way in disguise from New York through a region swarming with enemies. Brant had witnessed Howe's victories, and his observations had thoroughly convinced him of the power of England. Already he entertained dreams of a great Indian confederacy extending from Detroit to Montreal, independent of, but united in close alliance with, the English. His fiery eloquence stirred the Indians wherever he went, and when he arrived at Niagara in December he had already obtained many assurances of active support.

Butler decided to abide by his original instructions from Carleton, and received him coldly. After a very short stay, Brant resumed his agitation, travelling from village to village throughout the length and breadth of the league, not omitting to visit the hostile Oneidas, among whom he possessed some personal influence through his marriage into that tribe, urging them all to prepare for hostilities in the spring.

In Tryon County the situation of the remaining loyalists had steadily become less endurable. Their opponents, strengthened by the arrival of troops from New England, had obtained full control of all public affairs. They did not fail to make relentless use of their power. One of their first acts was to disarm Butler's tenants, and reorganize the militia under officers upon whom they could rely implicitly. The Articles of Association against the government were then presented to everybody. A few determined loyalists, such as Colonel Frey, the Reverend John Stuart, and Henry Hare, whose tragic fate will be noticed later, firmly refused to sign, and were imprisoned.

Sir John Johnson, surrounded by his tenants and strong in local influence, ventured to set them at defiance, telling the committee that he would rather lose his head than comply, and began secretly to form a regiment for the support of the government. His intentions were suspected, and General Schuyler with 4,000 men marched against him and disarmed the whole of his friends and tenants without firing a shot. Sir John was forced not only to sign a parole, but to give a bond for its observance. All his ready money was impounded, and a strict search made for hidden arms. Six leading men among the Highlanders and as many of the English and Dutch inhabitants were carried off as hostages. Although this was derisively termed by the loyalists

"Schuyler's peacock expedition," it really had very important results. All hope of a successful rising was ended, and the committees were henceforth at liberty to continue their oppression without fear of reprisals. All open dissent was instantly and severely punished.

For some months afterwards. Sir John Johnson was constantly annoyed by inquisitorial visits and required to give reasons for every movement. Finally, it was determined to make him a prisoner and remove the entire body of Highlanders from the county. Schuyler wrote a letter releasing him from his parole, and sent a New Jersey regiment to deliver it, and at the same time take him into custody. By some means Johnson was forewarned of this artful scheme and he determined to make his escape to Canada. Montreal was known to be still in the hands of the enemy, but a British fleet and army were said to be ascending the St. Lawrence. Hastily assembling 170 of his personal friends and tenants, he fled through the great Adirondac wilderness towards St. Regis, guided by a few faithful Mohawks. They had not had time to collect provisions, and during the nine days they were in the woods the whole party lived entirely upon wild onions, roots, and leaves of beech trees. When they arrived at Caughnawaga they were quite exhausted with fatigue and half dead with hunger. In a few days Johnson's force was swelled by Canadians and Indians to 500, and he crossed over to Montreal where he arrived the day after Sir Guy Carleton had recovered possession.

After his flight, the persecution of the miserable loyalists that remained behind was renewed with increased rigor. Of Guy Johnson's house only the walls were left standing. Johnson Hall was converted into a barracks and the contents carried off or destroyed. Lady Johnson and Mrs. Butler, with their children, were removed to Albany as hostages, together with the families of most of the Highlanders and other refugees. The committee remarked significantly, that as long as their wives and children were in their hands neither Johnson nor Butler would hardly dare to act against them, and if they did their families "would not be saved from the violence of the people."

That this might be no vain threat was clearly shown by a recent occurrence at Boston, where the wife and daughter of Captain Fenton, an obnoxious loyalist, had actually been tarred, feathered, and paraded through the streets by a mob of women. Colonel Frey, late member of the Provincial Assembly, and seventy more of the principal inhabitants, were deported to New England, Of the Highlanders, none were permitted to stay behind unless they would consent to give at least five hostages in every hundred persons, "on condition of being put to death if those that remained should take up arms or in any way assist the enemy."

For some months Lady Johnson was permitted to remain quietly with a relative in Albany, and found means to keep up a secret correspondence with her husband. But towards the end of the year, having learned that she was "a person of great art and political intrigue, and of great firmness of mind, and most warmly attached to that cause which is so inimical to the freedom and independence of the American States, and has done great injury to the American cause," the New York Convention gave orders that she should be removed to a safer place and more closely watched.

There were still numbers of quiet but steadfast loyalists in Albany and Tryon Counties, who were known to be biding their time to rise in arms. In the heart of the valley was the remnant of the Mohawks, surrounded by suspicious neighbours and narrowly watched, but ready to obey the summons of Johnson or Butler. Brant had not dared to approach nearer to them than Onondaga, and more than one letter written to prepare them for flight had been intercepted and only provoked stricter surveillance.

The Congress had not abandoned its hopes of enlisting some of the Indians in its service. During the summer of 1776, the Indian commissioners were authorized to engage any number of the Six Nations not exceeding 2000, and to promise them a substantial reward for every prisoner belonging to the regular army which they should make. It was suggested that they might even be bribed to surprise and deliver Fort Niagara into their hands by a promise of plunder of its contents. Such, however, was the temper of the Indians when they assembled, that the American commissioners from motives of policy, abstained from making any overtures to them, having been previously warned by their agents that these might produce an unfavourable impression.

Brant had continued his agitation with much success. In fact only the Oneidas had offered any serious opposition. Alarmed by his activity, the New York Convention engaged a party to kidnap him, but that project came to nothing. His own indiscretion caused him to meet with a not undeserved rebuff in an unexpected quarter. Elated by his favourable reception among the Senecas, he had written to the Indians of the Lake of Two Mountains dissuading them from serving under Sir Guy Carleton, and inviting them to join him instead, promising if they did that they should be allowed "to make war in their own way."

His letter was shown to Carleton, who was naturally annoyed at this bold attempt to interfere with his plans, and construed it to mean that Brant intended "an indiscriminate attack, wherein women and children, aged and infirm, innocent as well as the guilty, will be equally exposed to their fury." He instructed Butler in the strongest terms to prevent any such movement. In consequence Butler effectually put an end to Brant's design by refusing to supply him with powder and other articles, when he returned to Niagara to prepare for his campaign. Brant's indignation knew no bounds, and he left the place deeply offended with Butler, to whose "envy and jealousy" he solely attributed the refusal.

However, the policy of the British government with respect to the Indians had already undergone a change, and in May, 1777, Carleton received instructions to employ a body of the Six Nations in an invasion of the State of New York, taking due precautions "by placing proper persons at their head to conduct their parties and restrain them from committing violence on the well-affected and inoffensive inhabitants."

There is no evidence that Butler had ever advocated this step. At the end of the war he studiously avoided defending it, and contented himself by saying;

> Of the importance of the object I had no right to judge, either as a subject or a soldier. In both these capacities I submitted this to the consideration of my superiors, whose ideas of the policy, and even the necessity of conciliating the affections of the Indians and of steadily attaching them to the British government, will best appear from the unwearied pains which have been taken for that purpose from the first settlement of the colonies.

Only a month before, he had warmly urged the chiefs to take every means to prevent their people from committing any depredations on the frontiers. He was afterwards severely censured in their official correspondence by Col. Claus and Sir John Johnson, for having expended large sums among the Indians and yet kept them inactive while the enemy had taken possession of Fort Stanwix. They even hinted that he was then wavering in his allegiance. Yet all the time Butler had been faithfully and quietly executing his instructions, and when he received fresh instructions he carried them out with the same imperturbable fidelity and resolution as before.

On the 5th June, 1777, he received a letter from Carleton, directing him to collect as many Indians as possible and join Col. St. Leger, who had orders to advance from Montreal against Fort Stanwix, which stood on the present site of Rome, N.Y. The whole force was to be assembled at Oswego about the end of July.

Refugees had continued to arrive at Niagara from the Mohawk, many of them being persons of influence, and during the winter a Mr. Depue brought letters from seventy inhabitants of the Susquehanna, announcing their wish to enlist as Rangers under Butler's command. He had already encouraged them to join him at Niagara, and he next sent active agents among the Six Nations and Missassaugas to collect warriors for the proposed expedition. By the advice of the Senecas, the Indians at Detroit were also invited to send a contingent.

Before the middle of June Butler was able to announce that the agents of Congress had been baffled in their efforts to draw the Indians to the councils they had convened at Pittsburg and Albany, and to send the governor a list of five captains, nine lieutenants, and 75 Rangers, most of whom could speak some Indian language. Small parties of loyalists were daily arriving, with fresh tales of hardship and ruthless persecution. They reported that many more were merely waiting for a favourable opportunity to follow their example, and led Butler to believe that he could raise battalion of five hundred men very quickly. Equally favourable reports came in from other quarters. Mr. Jessup actually enlisted a hundred men near Albany, and Captain McDonnel of Sir John Johnson's regiment, brought off as many more from Schoharie to Crown Point.

On the other hand, the regiment of German riflemen detailed as part of St. Leger's force, with the exception of a single company, had not yet arrived at Quebec. The number of regular troops was accordingly diminished by more than a third, and amounted to less than 500, made up of detachments from four different corps. Sangerachta, the Seneca chief, headed about 200 of that nation, and Brant arrived at Oswego with as many gathered from several tribes. Other parties swelled the entire number of Indians collected there to 800 or 1000.

But it soon became manifest that a majority of these had not come with any intention of fighting. Col. Claus had arrived from England with a commission appointing him superintendent of all the Indians employed in the expedition. Carleton was consequently compelled to ratify the appointment, but he was so thoroughly well satisfied with Butler's conduct that he declined to displace him, but requested him to act as second in command. Butler loyally accepted the decision and consented to serve under his personal enemy.

Brant, with a few Indians, went forward cheerfully enough to assist a party of light infantry in surrounding the fort, but Butler was detained for several days by the remainder in needlessly prolonged conferences, and he did not succeed in bringing them up to the place until the 5th of August. At the very instant of his arrival, the startling information came in that 800 or 1000 of the Tryon County militia, under Gen. Herkimer, were on the march to relieve the garrison and would be within twelve miles of it that night. Half of St. Leger's small regular force was scattered along his line of communication for twenty miles, engaged in cutting a road and bringing up the artillery and stores.

Besides the Indians he had barely 250 men in camp. There were 750 in the fort, which was found to be unexpectedly strong. Butler could only muster 400 Indians, but he was at once directed to march with these to waylay the approaching enemy. Sir John Johnson volunteered to accompany him at the head of his light company. This, with a party of Rangers, made a party of eighty white soldiers. They advanced five miles, and halted for the night. In the morning their scouts announced that the enemy was approaching and only a few miles away. Even then it appears that Butler still hoped to avoid bloodshed and that the militia might be induced to disperse without coming to blows. He may have had reason to suspect that many of them were apathetic or even friendly. Gen. Herkimer's own brother, brother-in-law, and nephew were at that moment serving as officers with the Indians.

Other families were divided in a similar manner. Butler accordingly proposed that the relieving force should be summoned to lay down its arms and disband. But Brant and the Indians generally were eager for battle, and hotly opposed this. Their opinion prevailed and the whole force moved forward and selected a position near the "Orisca field," where the road leading to Fort Stanwix crossed a marsh in the bottom of a deep ravine, by means of a rude causeway. Dense thickets on both sides of the narrow wagon-track made this an ideal spot for an ambuscade. On the crest of the further slope, Johnson's light infantry was stationed across the road to block the way at the proper moment,, while the Indians were hidden among the thickets, with instructions to gain the rear of the advancing column and entirely surround it before beginning the attack.

They had not been there long before the creaking of the ponderous ox-wagons, in which they conveyed their baggage and provisions, announced the approach of Herkimer's force. When they reached the marsh the flanking parties closed in upon the main body to cross the causeway, and the attenuated column advanced heedlessly into the jaws of the trap prepared for them. During his march Herkimer had been joined by sixty Oneidas, but even these practised woodsmen had failed to notice any sign of danger. The causeway was already hopelessly choked with their unwieldy wagons, when the eagerness of some drunken Indians precipitated the attack and saved the rear-guard from the fate that overtook the rest of the column.

The first deliberate volley that burst upon them from a distance of a very few yards was terribly destructive. Elated by the sight and maddened with the smell of blood and gunpowder, many of the Indians rushed from their coverts to complete the victory with spear and hatchet. The rear-guard promptly ran away in a wild panic. Of the remainder many were slaughtered almost without resistance, but some cool-headed fellows kept up a running fight until the clouds burst in a terrific rainstorm, which put an end to the further use of firearms. Even then the pursuit was continued until tidings came that the garrison had made a sortie and taken possession of part of the camp. Butler estimated that the militia left five hundred of their number on the field, of whom at least two hundred were killed.

The Indians butchered many after they had surrendered, in revenge for the comparatively heavy loss they had themselves sustained through their unwonted recklessness in engaging in a hand to hand fight. Thirty-three Indians were killed and twenty-nine wounded. More than half of these were Senecas. Captains Hare and Wilson of the Rangers were killed, and Private David Secord was wounded; one officer of Johnson's regiment was killed and two were wounded.

Decisive as this success appeared at the time, it proved a barren victory. The fort was too strong to be taken by assault, the garrison remained defiant, and the besiegers had no artillery capable of making a breach in the defences. As usual after a successful battle, the Indians began to disperse with whatever booty they had obtained. Those who remained were surly and dispirited by the plunder of their camp during the sortie, by which they lost their blankets and much of their clothing, "having gone in their shirts as naked to action." When it became known that a much larger and better disciplined force, under

Benedict Arnold, was on its way to relieve the place, St. Leger had no alternative but to raise the siege and return to Montreal.

Butler went to Quebec to settle his accounts, taking with him three of the principal chiefs to present them to the governor. He then renewed his proposal to raise a battalion of Rangers to serve with the Indians, to which Sir Guy Carleton readily consented, and furnished him with "beating orders" for the enlistment of eight companies, each composed of a captain, a lieutenant, three sergeants, three corporals, and fifty privates. Two of these companies were to be formed of "people speaking the Indian language and acquainted with their customs and manner of making war," and were to receive four shillings, New York currency, a day. The remaining companies, "to be composed of people well acquainted with the woods, in consideration of the fatigue they are liable to undergo," were to receive two shillings a day. The whole were required to clothe and arm themselves entirely at their own expense. This was considered extremely high pay, and it was subsequently estimated by General Haldimand that these eight companies of Rangers cost the government as much as twenty companies of regular infantry.

On the same day, (Sept. 15th,) Col. Butler received instructions to march with such Rangers as he had already enlisted or could enlist at once, and as large a body of Indians as could be collected without exposing their country to invasion, and form a junction with Gen. Burgoyne's army. On his way to Niagara he received much discouraging information. The Indians had protested warmly against the withdrawal of the British troops from Oswego, saying that they were being abandoned to their enemies contrary to the assurances they had received.

Sickness prevailed to such an extent at Niagara that the garrison was reduced to seventy-five men fit for duty. Schuyler had promptly seized the opportune moment, when the Indians were still fuming with disappointment, and invited them to meet him at the German Flats, "to settle what was past and renew their former chain of friendship," adding that he "did not blame them for what had happened, but he had long ago told them that Col. Butler would lead them to ruin." He requested that they would "deliver him up and not follow his wicked counsels anymore." He announced his intention of taking possession of Oswego, and declared that if he found that Butler had gone to Niagara, he would follow him thither, and if he had gone to Montreal he would intercept him on his return.

A letter from a trader at Niagara informed Butler that some of the Senecas were much displeased with him, and that the loyal chiefs were alarmed and anxious for his speedy return.

At the same time Claus and Johnson were steadily endeavouring to undermine his influence by every means within their reach. They criticised his actions with undisguised rancour, and confidently predicted that he would not succeed in enlisting many Rangers.

Upon arriving at Carleton Island, at the foot of Lake Ontario, Butler learned that the Oneidas, Onondagas and Tuscaroras had actually accepted the hatchet tendered them by General Schuyler, and had proved their hostility by making prisoners of some loyalists passing through their country. His son Walter and two other officers of the Indian department were confined at Albany, heavily ironed, and otherwise cruelly treated. He had intended to proceed overland from Oswego to Niagara, passing through all the principal Indian villages on his way and engaging warriors for his proposed expedition. This design he was then forced to abandon as being too dangerous, and went on by water.

At Niagara he was overtaken by the astounding intelligence of the surrender of Burgoyne's whole army. Consequently the movement he had been instructed to make was no longer practicable. Most of his Rangers had marched overland to the Susquehanna after the siege of Fort Stanwix was raised, with orders to drive cattle from the settlements to Niagara for the maintenance of the garrison, but nothing had been heard of them since the forest had swallowed them.

Presently Joseph Brant arrived, still resolute and hopeful. He had attended a general meeting of the whole confederacy at Onondaga, at which there had been a very stormy debate over their future policy. The majority of the Senecas and Cayugas were still friendly, and at their suggestion Butler boldly summoned the other tribes to come to him and deliver up the hatchet they had accepted from Schuyler, adding, significantly, that none but his real friends need appear. He must have been agreeably surprised at the success of this measure. All the chiefs of the Tuscaroras and Onondagas obeyed very promptly. They surrendered the hatchet and war-belt they had received, and humbly promised to follow his advice in future.

A trusty courier instantly sped off through the woods towards New York with a message for the commander of the British forces on the Hudson, announcing that they were ready for action, and asking for instructions. "Our friends," Butler said in conclusion, "are determined to be so, in the worst of times."

His former agent, Depue, again hurried to the Susquehanna to seek fresh recruits, and hasten the return of the Rangers already there. Loyalists continued to arrive, and by the middle of December the first company of Rangers was completed, and Butler expected to form two more upon the return of his recruiting officers. Then followed tidings of an unexpected disaster. The party of Rangers detached from Oswego to the Susquehanna was conducted by James Secord. After prolonged wanderings they were surprised by an overwhelming force, and thirty taken prisoners. The remainder dispersed, and several had returned to their former homes.

At the same time the Senecas and Cayugas were seriously alarmed by repeated rumours of an attack upon their villages by the masterful Connecticut settlers in Wyoming, who had already set the State Government of Pennsylvania at complete defiance. Butler's force had then increased to 125, and he immediately prepared to march to their support. These tribes gave him the strongest assurances of their fidelity, and he mentioned that with the object of strengthening their determination they had resorted to "some superstitious rites which have often produced effects upon a fierce and barbarous people."

Their fears proved groundless at the time, and the Senecas haughtily refused to receive a belt sent to them from Schuyler, replying that the blood of their kinsmen was still reeking from the ground and that he had been the cause of shedding it. Their war-parties then fell upon the border settlements of Pennsylvania, lying between the east branch of the Susquehanna and the Kiskismenitas Creek, and in a few days reduced them to smouldering ruins, driving the unfortunate inhabitants that escaped into the numerous small forts built for their protection. It is admitted that the rough frontiersmen of that quarter had given the Indians abundant provocation for several years past, for which dreadful retribution was then exacted.

> The inhabitants, (said Timothy Pickering in a letter to Washington), appear, many of them, to be a wild, ungovernable race, little less savage than their tawny neighbours, and by savage barbarities in fact provoked them to revenge, but the innocent are now involved in one common calamity with the guilty, and all are greatly disheartened.

McKee had escaped from Pittsburg and safely arrived at Detroit, where he took charge of the Indian department. Everywhere there were undoubted signs of reaction. Soon after McKee's flight from Pittsburg a plot to surprise the fort was discovered and many of the inhabitants were imprisoned. Thirty desperate men from the neighbouring country then attempted to make their way to Detroit, but some were killed and others driven back by the Indians. Governor Hamilton was informed that two hundred persons were prepared to come away in a body if they could obtain a safe conduct through the Indian territory.

During the winter, the Senecas carefully abstained from molesting the frontier of New York until they found an opportunity of removing such of their friends as might be exposed to retaliation, when they told Butler that they meant "to strike in a body." This information caused him to march among them with the object of controlling and directing their movements in accordance with his instructions, and of meeting various parties of recruits which he learned were on their way to join him. Letters from the frontier informed him that one officer had enlisted nearly a hundred men, and that others had likewise been moderately successful. He confidently anticipated that he would be able to complete his battalion immediately after reaching the settlements.

Many of his best recruits were drawn from the east branch of the Susquehanna, where all persons suspected of loyalist leanings were keenly persecuted. Accordingly, he began his march from Niagara on the 2nd of May, 1778, and after holding a council with the Indians at Canadasaga, the principal village of the Senecas, situated near the present site of Geneva, N.Y., fixed his headquarters at Unadilla on the Susquehanna. The white inhabitants of that village were all loyalists. There were two grist mills in the vicinity which could be used to grind flour for his force.

It was equally near the frontiers of the three States of New York, New Jersey, and Pennsylvania, which he could thus menace and alarm at once, and he could easily "fall upon such part of New York" as would enable him to join Sir Henry Clinton whenever he received orders for that purpose. In the meantime, it was his intention to protect the Indian villages from attack and to make war sustain war by taking his supplies from the enemy, sweeping along and breaking up their "back settlements" as he did so. In this way he anticipated that he might create a diversion of considerable importance in favour of Clinton or Howe, in their operations nearer the seaboard.

He found the Senecas suffering severely from want of both food and clothing through the stoppage of the usual channels of trade by the war, but still resolute in their hostility to the Americans. They had sent spies to the council called to meet at Johnstown by Schuyler, as Commissioner of Congress, and La Fayette as representative of the King of France. It was attended by 700 Indians, chiefly Oneidas and Onondagas. Schuyler and La Fayette addressed them in turn, assuring them of the favour and protection of Congress and its ally. A liberal quantity of presents was then distributed and the Indians announced their intention of remaining neutral.

The officers of Congress in the State of New York had not been deceived by the inactivity of the Senecas during the winter. Stockades were built in every settlement. As they seldom ventured to put much dependence on the local militia, these posts were generally occupied by detachments of Continental troops from Massachusetts, New Jersey, or distant parts of New York. Four hundred women and children belonging to the families of the principal loyalist refugees were seized and confined at Albany as hostages for the safety of the frontier. Butler's entire family was then in the hands of his bitterest enemies, and his eldest son was reported to be slowly dying from the effects of his treatment. There was scarcely an officer in the Rangers or the Indian department that had not some near relative among the captives.

Every party of fugitives had some fresh story of outrage and cruelty to relate. Several loyalist recruiting officers had been taken and unceremoniously hanged. Still, recruits continue to come in, burning with a fierce desire for retaliation, but generally ragged, footsore, and weak with hunger and travel. Doubtless there was some exaggeration in their version of their wrongs, but there could be no dispute as to the leading facts. " The confiscation of the effects of the disaffected," General Roberdeau, a member of Congress, reported, "is very irregular, and the brutality offered to the wives and children of some of them, as I am informed, in taking from them even their wearing apparel, is shocking."

These fugitives had little knowledge of drill or military discipline, but the chief requisites of a good Ranger being, as General Haldimand subsequently remarked, "to shoot well, to march well, and to endure privation and fatigue," they came well schooled in these respects, and many minor forms of parade could readily be dispensed with in service.

Butler's first step was to send Brant and Lieut. Barent Frey with a small party of Rangers and Indians to bring away the remainder of the

Mohawks from their villages, where they were still forcibly detained. This was a difficult and dangerous enterprise, which was very adroitly executed, Butler was cheered at the same time by the unexpected appearance of his son Walter, who had escaped from his Albany prison, where he was lying under sentence of death. He had safely travelled more than two hundred miles on foot and horseback through a country abounding in enemies. Still too sick and weak to take command of the company in the Rangers to which he had been appointed, he was despatched to Quebec to regain health and obtain arms and clothing for the corps.

From Unadilla it would be a matter of ease to strike swiftly either at Cherry Valley, Schoharie, or Wyoming, all populous advanced settlements protected by forts, occupied by strong detachments of regular soldiers, and distinguished by the revolutionary fervour of the inhabitants, who were chiefly recent immigrants from New England. From all of these places the American armies had already drawn some recruits and supplies of inestimable value, and it became an object of no small importance to destroy the coming harvest before it could be lodged in their magazines. The Senecas were particularly anxious to expel the Wyoming settlers, against whom they cherished a long-standing grudge. Brant and Frey were detached with eighty men to alarm and harass Cherry Valley and Schoharie, while Butler, with the main body, proceeded in that direction.

Moving with bewildering rapidity along the skirts of the settlements, Brant and Frey made a hasty descent here and there, and kept a great stretch of country in constant alarm. Twice they were pursued by small bodies of Continental troops, reinforced by the local militia, and twice they turned upon their pursuers and by a well-planned ambush fairly annihilated them with scarcely any loss to their own party. After two months of this guerrilla warfare they were able to report that they had killed or taken 294 men in arms, and desolated a great part of the Schoharie valley, even forcing some of the inhabitants to take refuge in Schenectady.

The valley of Wyoming or the County of Westmoreland, as it was officially named, contained a very thriving and populous settlement, entirely composed of emigrants from Connecticut. Yet it was by no means the Arcadia that has been pictured. On the contrary, for ten years back it had been a scene of strife and violence, and the inhabitants had seized and held their farms by force of arms alone. Rival land companies had waged an obstinate struggle for possession of the narrow but fertile tract of alluvial soil skirting the river, during which small armies were organized, forts built and besieged, many houses burnt, and several persons killed. In this conflict, William Caldwell, one of Butler's captains, had served his apprenticeship in arms, and many of the Rangers were Pennsylvanians who had been expelled from their holdings by the triumphant invaders and had seen their houses wrapped in flames as they fled.

The population had increased so rapidly that it was estimated at 6,000, congregated in a valley twenty-five miles in length and nowhere more than three in breadth. Many thousand bushels of grain had been shipped during the past year for the supply of the Continental army near Philadelphia, and it was anticipated that the harvest then ripening would furnish a still greater quantity for the same purpose. The inhabitants were, with few exceptions, warm partisans of the Revolution, and had already sent two companies of riflemen to serve under Washington. These had been recently recalled for the defence of their homes and were accompanied by a small detachment of Continental infantry under Colonel Zebulon Butler, The magistrates had lately shown their zeal by the prosecution of some persons living further up the river, who were accused of being loyalists. Thirty of these were seized and committed to jail in Connecticut. The remainder were summarily ejected, and most of them fled to Unadilla and joined the Rangers.

The Indians contended that they were still the rightful owners of the lands occupied by the Wyoming people. They had protested fruitlessly for more than twenty years against the settlement of the valley. Sangerachta, the Seneca chief, had acted as the spokesman of one deputation that had been sent to Connecticut to remonstrate. The justice of their claim was then generally admitted, and the movement delayed until the disturbances preceding the Revolution afforded a favourable opportunity for reviving it. Hamilton, the Governor of Pennsylvania, declared that "nothing is more certain than that these lands do yet belong to these nations, having never, that I heard of, been openly and fairly purchased of them."

The Connecticut Company next attempted, without success, to bribe Sir Wm. Johnson by an offer of half their interest. "I refused their offer," Johnson said, "with the slight it deserved, and gave them my opinion of the whole affair, and also told them the unhappy consequences that would follow should they, as so often hinted, force a settlement in those parts." He added that he did not believe the Six

Nations would ever consent to a settlement on their war-path and best hunting-ground." The land-hunger in that "teeming hive, Connecticut," was too powerful to be long withstood, and the unhappy squatters were now doomed to suffer the *"wrong that amendeth wrong."*

Aside from the land question, the Senecas had a more recent cause for irritation. In the autumn of the preceding year a party from their tribe had been invited to visit the settlement. Liquor was given them there. Some of them got drunk and uttered vague threats. They were seized, and had been detained as hostages ever since. In April, 1777, the chiefs of the tribe received a message from Colonel Denniston and Judge Jenkins in the name of the inhabitants, inviting them to a council. Mindful of former treachery, the Indians applied to Col. Butler for the assistance of a body of troops to enable them to go in such force as to secure the release of the prisoners.

Accordingly, Butler was instructed to accompany them with his whole force. Before this could be done, the Indians were further exasperated by an indefensible act of cruelty. A few of their people having approached within five miles of Wyoming, were stealthily attacked by a scouting party from the settlement, and two men and a woman killed and scalped.

Floating down the Susquehanna in boats and rafts to the great bend at the Three Islands, Butler then marched swiftly through the woods with 200 Rangers and 300 Indians. On the last day of June he encamped on the summit of a high hill, from which he looked down on the greater part of the valley. His scouts brought in a few prisoners, and at night he was joined by two loyalists. From these men it was learned that his approach had been discovered, and that in addition to sixty Continentals the entire militia of the settlement, numbering eight hundred men, had been assembled in the various forts.

Of these there were eight or ten, the three largest being on the same side of the river as his camp. Next morning the Indians sent a message to Col. Denniston informing him that they had come in consequence of his invitation, and were prepared to speak with him either as friends or foes. The defiant answer was returned that the inhabitants were determined to fight, and "would have all their scalps before night."

Butler at once marched within view of Wintemute's Fort, and sent Lieut. John Turney of the Rangers to summon it. Terms were soon arranged by which the garrison agreed to surrender the place with all their arms and stores, and engaged not to bear arms again during the war, on the sole condition that their lives should be preserved. Jenkins' fort next capitulated on the same terms. Forty Fort, the remaining garrison on that side of the river, was then summoned, but after long deliberation the terms were rejected.

Two days had been consumed in this way, and on the morning of the 3rd July, parties sent out by Butler to collect cattle reported that the militia were assembling in great numbers near Forty Fort, and apparently preparing for an attack. At this the Indians rejoiced greatly, and prepared for action with alacrity, saying that they would at least be on an equal footing with them in the woods. Shortly after noon four or five hundred men were seen advancing slowly along the river. This force was composed of the entire detachment of Continental infantry and Wyoming riflemen under Colonel Zebulon Butler, a veteran soldier who had served through the French war and at the siege of Havana, and the greater part of the 24th regiment of Connecticut militia commanded by Colonel Denniston himself. For many years these militiamen had been armed and carefully trained, and in the land-war they had easily routed their antagonists.

Caldwell, who was destroying Jenkins' fort, was recalled, and at four o'clock, when the enemy was still about a mile away, Butler directed Fort Wintemute to be set on fire. Supposing that this was the forerunner of a retreat, the Americans pushed forward rapidly. He then posted his men in a "fine open wood," extending from an impenetrable marsh to the river, the Indians being stationed on the right in six distinct parties, and ordered them to lie flat on the ground and reserve their fire until a signal was given by the Seneca chief. He laid aside his military hat, tied a handkerchief around his head, and taking a rifle, posted himself in the centre of the Rangers.

After they had passed the burning stockade, the enemy deployed and advanced in line until within two hundred yards of the Rangers' position, when they discovered them and began firing. They had fired three rounds without receiving a shot in reply, and gradually advanced within a hundred yards, when Sangerachta gave a shrill whoop, which was repeated by each band of Indians in succession and prolonged by the Rangers. This was succeeded by a deliberate and deadly volley. Already the Indians had turned the enemy's left flank by creeping along the margin of the marsh, and the militia in that part of the line gave way in a sudden panic. The Indians darted forward to cut off their retreat, and drove them in confusion towards the river. After that they offered but little resistance, and a merciless pursuit began. Many tried to swim the river, and were shot or drowned in the act.

Our fire was so close and well-directed, (Butler said in his letter to Col. Bolton), that the affair was soon over, not lasting above half an hour from the time they gave the first fire till their flight. In this action were taken 227 scalps and only five prisoners. The Indians were so exasperated with their loss at Fort Stanwix last year that it was with difficulty I could save the lives of these few. Col. Denniston, who came in next day with a minister and four others to treat for the remainder of the settlement of West-moreland, told me they had lost one colonel, two majors, seven captains, thirteen lieutenants, eleven ensigns and 268 privates. On our side we lost one Indian killed, two Rangers and eight Indians wounded.

Only sixty of the entire body that marched out to give battle are said to have escaped, of whom fourteen were Continentals. It is certain that Butler strongly disapproved of this wholesale slaughter. This story was told by a wounded officer who escaped by secreting himself in a thicket. After dark he heard the sound of footsteps, and two men, whom he recognized as Butler himself and one of his officers, passed so near his hiding place that he could overhear snatches of their conversation.

"It has been a sore day for the Yankees," the younger man said.

"It has indeed," replied Butler sadly, "blood enough has been shed."

The three forts at Laruwanak, on the opposite side of the river, surrendered at the first summons next morning, and a deputation headed by Col. Denniston and a clergyman came from Forty Fort to beg for terms for the rest of the settlement. The few surviving regulars had fled from the valley during the night. Already the mills and many farmhouses were in flames, and an immense drove of cattle had been collected as plunder by the Indians.

Butler readily agreed to grant the same conditions that he had offered before the battle, and even consented that Forty Fort should remain standing as a place of refuge for the women and children. As a measure of precaution he insisted that all spirits should be destroyed before the stores were delivered, and more than one of the prisoners remembered to the end of their lives his constant efforts to prevent the Indians from plundering, and even from taunting the inhabitants with their defeat.

Those who fled from the valley told a far different story of death and desolation, which their fears prompted them to embellish with blood-curdling and wholly imaginary details. This tale of horror was eagerly circulated to throw odium upon the loyalists, and has been repealed with little variation down to the present day. Undoubtedly there was a "massacre" at Wyoming, but it was of strong men flying from a lost battle, and not of prisoners or helpless women and children as they represented.

By the final capitulation it was agreed that all the forts should be utterly demolished, the Continental stores surrendered, and that none of the inhabitants should again bear arms. The prisoners on both sides were to be liberated, and it was further stipulated by Butler that "properties taken from the people called Tories up the river be made good, and that they are to remain in peaceable possession of their farms and unmolested in a free trade through this state as far as lies in their power." On his part, he promised to "use his utmost influence that the property of the inhabitants shall be preserved entire to them."

He afterwards assorted in the most solemn language that these conditions were faithfully observed by him, while it is not denied that they were violated by Col. Denniston and others, who appeared in arms before the year was ended. In his letter to Col. Bolton already cited, written from Laruwanak on the 12th July, Butler said;

> But what gives me the sincerest satisfaction is that I can, with great truth, assure you that in the destruction of the settlement not a single person was hurt except such as were in arms, to these, in truth, the Indians gave no quarter. The officers and men of the Rangers have supported themselves through hunger and fatigue with great cheerfulness.

Miner, the local historian of Wyoming, practically corroborates Butler's statement, although with evident trepidation as to the probable consequences of telling the truth.

> Even now, (1840) it is not without some fear of giving offence we draw of him what we believe to be a just outline. It is certain he could have commanded much more severe conditions. The settlement was wholly at his mercy. No one can deny that the capitulation on its face was in a high degree honourable and favourable to Col. Denniston. Col. Franklin confirms the statement of Mrs. Myers, that Butler exerted himself to restrain the savages, seemed deeply hurt when unable to do so, and of-

fered, when furnished with a list of property, to make it good.

He describes one grim deed of which Butler himself made no mention. When the garrison of Forty Fort marched out, Butler stood at the gateway and recognized one Boyd, a deserter from Niagara. "Boyd!" he exclaimed, "Go to that tree!"

"I hope, sir," Boyd faltered, "that you will consider me a prisoner of war."

"Go to that tree, sir!" Butler repeated sternly.

The trembling wretch obeyed, and at a signal from their commander a volley was fired by a party of Rangers, and he fell dead. This, Miner states, was the only life taken after the capitulation was signed.

From the recollections of survivors, he succeeded in constructing a life-like portrait of Butler as he appeared to them.

A fat man, below the middle stature yet active; through the rough visage of the warrior showing a rather agreeable than forbidding aspect. Care sat upon his brow. Speaking quickly, he repeated his words when excited. Decision, firmness, courage were undoubted characteristics of the man.

The fate of Wyoming spread terror along the border, and Butler took advantage of the general panic to send a party to destroy the settlement on the Lackawaxen branch of the Deleware. For many days the roads and the rivers were covered for miles by throngs of people flying from their homes. The adjacent counties were nearly deserted, and Sunbury became the frontier post on the west branch of the Susquehanna. It was asserted that Butler might have advanced without opposition as fur as Carlisle.

(An eye witness said), I never in my life saw such scenes of distress. The river and the roads down it were covered with men, women and children, flying for their lives, many without any property at all and none who have not left the greatest part of it.

(Another writes of) 700 Indians, all armed in the most formidable manner. Every one of them, exclusive of guns and *tomahawks*, hath a large *spontoon* and as soon as engaged rushes on in a most dreadful manner.

The Executive Council of Pennsylvania instantly ordered two regiments of regulars and 1800 militia to march to the defence of the frontier. Much of the harvest elsewhere was destroyed in consequence, and the diversion of so many troops to this quarter unquestionably hampered the movements of their main army.

Struck down at Tioga a few days later by a violent attack of fever and ague accompanied by "rheumatism in the head," Butler was forced to seek relief at Niagara, leaving Caldwell in command of the Rangers, with instructions to march at once to Oquaga and inform the Indians that he had come to assist in the defence of their border villages, and conduct any offensive movement he considered practicable. An officer and a few Rangers were to accompany every party of Indians sent out to reconnoitre and harass the frontier.

> I would have you give orders, (Butler continued), to every party you send out to burn and destroy everything they possibly can. If we can prevent the enemy getting in their grain, their general army, already much distressed, must disperse and their country full an easy prey. You are to enlist as many able-bodied men as you can, who are recommended for their loyalty.

A memorandum of the distribution of the Rangers early in September indicates the vast extent of country covered by their operations at this time.

> Captain Caldwell of the Rangers. Captain Powell of the Indian department, and Mr. Joseph Brant, are at Aughquaga, employed in scouting from there to the Deleware River, as low as the Minnesinks and to Schoharie, as well to annoy the enemy as to gain intelligence. Mr. Pawling is also detached from Aughquaga with thirty Rangers and a number of Indians to Wyalusing, upon the Susquehanna, with directions to scout as low as Wyoming, to watch the motions of the rebels said to be assembling there. Mr. John Young, detached from Aughquaga with thirty Rangers, is constantly scouting towards the German Flats and Cherry Valley. Captain Johnson, from the Seneca country, keeps continual parties of Indians out from thence to the west branch of the Susquehanna and Juniata. Mr. Adams, of the Indian department at Carleton Island is employed in scouting towards Fort Stanwix. The chiefs of Upper Seneca keep an attentive eye on Fort Pitt. The main body of the Rangers is at Aughquaga and neighbourhood, ready, when joined by the Indians, for an incursion to the enemy's frontier or to defend the Indian country.

Although the force at his disposal did not exceed 600 Rangers, and Indians, it appears that a continuous chain of scouting parties was maintained during the summer from Lake Ontario to the Ohio.

While Butler was engaged in harrying Wyoming, Sir John Johnson was at the governor's elbow in Quebec maliciously whispering that he would fail to do anything worthy of note. We have his own evidence on this point. On the 16th July he wrote to Clans with evident satisfaction;

He (Haldimand) asked me yesterday what Butler would be about all this time; that he thought he could have struck a blow ere now. I told him I thought I might venture to assure him that it was not his intention, that he would remain where he was or thereabouts till he could join the army from New York with safety, or till it was too late to do anything.

During the time Caldwell held command a tragic event occurred, which occasioned profound discontent among the Rangers. A number of unknown men had offered themselves from time to time for enlistment. Some, it was subsequently discovered, were actually spies in the enemy's service. A single traitor might easily accomplish the destruction of the entire corps. During his advance upon Wyoming, Butler had accordingly issued a standing order that if any man should attempt to desert he must be instantly pursued and shot on the spot. Shortly after their arrival at Oquaga two men from the Susquehanna asked leave to visit their families. Caldwell peremptorily refused.

Taking advantage of an opportunity when on guard at the "Indian Castle," they stole quietly away with their arms, after destroying the arms of the rest of the guard. This, of course, was an unpardonable offence. Caldwell sent out a party which soon overtook the fugitives and shot them at sight. But their friends and relatives stubbornly refused to believe that they had actually intended to desert, and continued to manifest their sympathy for the offenders in various ways.

Late in August Walter Butler returned from Quebec, bringing with him Lieut. John McDonnel of the 84th Regt., or Royal Highland Emigrants, a young officer already highly distinguished for activity and courage, who, finding there was little prospect of active employment with his own regiment, had obtained leave to serve with the Rangers. In after years McDonnel became known in civil life as member for Glengarry, and speaker of the first Legislative Assembly of Upper Canada. As senior captain, Butler superseded Caldwell, and McDonnel was put in command of a company. Caldwell was then detached with 200 Rangers and 160 Indians against the German Flats, where there were two large forts occupied by a Continental regiment.

Advancing swiftly through the woods from Unadilla, he met and captured a party of Oneidas. He had good reason to suspect that these Indians were scouts in the enemy's service, but his own Indians insisted that they should be liberated. A party of white scouts was next encountered. Three men were instantly shot, but the sole survivor outran all his pursuers and got off. At night a heavy rain began, and the darkness became so complete that Caldwell was forced to halt on the very outskirts of the settlement instead of advancing upon the fort as he had intended. The rain was falling in torrents when daylight returned, but he instantly gave the order to move on, still hoping to surprise the garrison, but every house was found deserted. The entire population had taken refuge in the forts. The melancholy work of destruction began. How thoroughly it was performed may be judged from Caldwell's own brief description.

> We destroyed all the grain and buildings on the German Flats, from William Tygert's to Fort Herkimer on the south side of the river, and from Adam Staring's to Wydeck's beyond Canada Creek on the north side, except the church and Fort Dayton, and drove off a great many cows and oxen, horses and mares. The oxen were all large New England cattle, kept on the flats for the use of the Continental troops, and we took them out of the enclosure at Fort Dayton within pistol-shot of the fort.

The inhabitants reported that five mills and 120 other buildings were destroyed, and 826 cattle killed or driven off.

On his return to Unadilla, Caldwell had the mortification to learn that the Oneidas he had liberated, had plundered the loyalists there and carried off some prisoners, among them two sick Rangers. This was followed by a formidable inroad by a body of regulars and militia, estimated at 1400, under Col. Hartley, piloted by Denniston and others who had surrendered at Wyoming. Another force from Schoharie advanced at the same time upon Oquaga and Unadilla. They burnt both those villages with the houses and mills of the Scottish loyalists in the vicinity. By this raid the Young family, which had already furnished Butler with two active officers, suffered severely in property. Hartley ascended the Susquehanna as far as Tioga, desolating the farms of many loyalists as he advanced, and burnt the Indian village there.

He then sent a written message to the chiefs of Chemung, a few miles distant, accusing them of killing women and children and torturing prisoners. He threatened to waste their country with "fire and sword" if they delayed to sue for peace. Captain Butler had retired to Canadasaga, where he was joined by Caldwell with the Rangers. The Senecas rapidly assembled 400 men, leaving only their women and children to take care of their villages. Convinced that if the Six Nations "were forced to a neutrality, Niagara would be in great danger," Col. Bolton sent a few volunteers from the 8th to join him. Finding himself at the head of 800 men, Butler prepared to attack Hartley, when he retreated with every sign of haste. His rear-guard was fiercely assailed and lost fifteen men, but carried off five Indian scalps.

Butler saw that the favourable moment for a counterstroke had arrived. While strong parties dogged the steps of the retreating enemy, he marched with 200 Rangers, a small party of the 8th and 321 Indians, against Cherry Valley, where they had long been forming magazines and collecting cattle. The forts there were occupied by Alden's Massachusetts regiment and the inhabitants generally were bitterly hostile, and even ostentatiously defiant of the Indians.

On the night of the 9th November, while yet twenty miles from their destination, a scout of nine men sent out by the garrison was surprised and taken. From them it was learned that the commandant had been warned of their approach by an Oneida, and that the Continentals numbered 300 and the militia 150. They also stated that most of the officers usually slept in a house a quarter of a mile outside the fort, attended by a strong guard.

After an exhausting march next day through a blinding now-storm and over ground covered with deep wet snow and mud, Butler halted his men at dark, in a pinewood, which afforded them some shelter, six miles from Cherry Valley. He assembled the chiefs and proposed that as soon as the moon rose, they should resume their march and surround the house occupied by the officers, while he made a rush upon the fort with the Rangers. They readily assented, but before the time appointed arrived it began to rain violently, and they obstinately refused to move until daybreak.

It was then arranged that Capt. McDonnel with 50 picked Rangers and some Indians should storm the house, while Butler with the remainder assailed the fort. Without tents, blankets or fires, they spent a sleepless night cowering beneath the pines, and were glad to move as soon as day appeared. They had approached unperceived within a mile of the fort, by passing through a dense swamp, when the Indians in front fired at two men cutting wood. One fell dead; the other, though bleeding, ran for his life and the entire body of Indians set up a whoop and followed at full speed.

Unhappily the Rangers had just been halted to fix flints and load their rifles, and the Indians obtained a long start. The Continental officers attempted to escape to the fort but only two or three reached it. The colonel, five other officers and twenty soldiers, were killed on the way and the lieutenant-colonel, three subalterns, and ten privates were taken. The colours of the regiment were abandoned in the house and burnt in it.

The garrison of the fort was fully alarmed, and opened a fierce fire of artillery and small arms. The Rangers seized and burnt a detached block-house, and fired briskly at the loop-holes in the palisades for ten minutes, when Butler saw with horror and consternation that the Indians had set their officers at defiance, and dispersed in every direction to kill and plunder.

Their wretched misconduct forced him to collect all the Rangers into a compact body on an eminence near the principal entrance to the fort, to oppose a sally by the garrison, which then undoubtedly outnumbered them considerably. There he was obliged to remain inactive all day under a ceaseless, chilling rain, while blazing houses and shrieks of agony told their pitiful tale in the settlement below. At nightfall he marched a mile down the valley and encamped. He then struggled with indifferent success to rescue the prisoners. Those surrendered were placed next the camp fires and protected by his whole force.

Next morning most of the Indians and the feeblest men among the Rangers were sent away with a huge drove of captured cattle for the supply of the garrison at Niagara, and McDonnel and Brant, with 60 Rangers and 50 Indians, swept the valley from end to end, ruthlessly burning every building and stack in sight, while Butler, with the remainder, again stood guard at the gate of the fort. He hoped that this appalling spectacle would provoke the garrison to sally out and fight, but the lesson of Wyoming had not been lost on them, and they continued to look on from the walls in silent fury. Another great herd of cattle was collected, and Butler leisurely began his retreat, having had only two Rangers and three Indians wounded during the expedition.

He did not disguise the dark side of the story in his letter to Col.

Bolton of the 17th November.

I have much to lament, (he said), that notwithstanding my utmost precautions to save the women and children, I could not prevent some of them falling victims to the fury of the savages. They have carried off many of the inhabitants and killed more, among them Colin Cloyd, a very violent rebel. I could not prevail on the Indians to leave the women and children behind, though the second morning Captain Johnson (to whose knowledge of the Indians and address in managing them I am much indebted) and I got them to permit twelve, who were loyalists, and whom I concealed, with the humane assistance of Mr. Joseph Brant and Captain Jacobs of Ochquaga, to return.

The death of the women and children on this occasion may, I believe, be truly ascribed to the rebels having falsely accused the Indians of cruelty at Wyomen. This has much exasperated them, and they are still more incensed at finding that the colonel and those who had then laid down their arms, soon after marching into their country intending to destroy their villages, and they declared that they would be no more accused falsely of fighting the enemy twice, meaning they would in future give no quarter.

In addition to those mentioned here, he actually set at liberty seven men, ten women, and thirty-two children, leaving with them a letter addressed to General Schuyler, in which he said:—

I am induced by humanity to permit the prisoners whose names are enclosed to remain behind, lest the inclemency of the season and their helpless and naked condition should prove fatal. I hope you will allow Mrs. Butler and her family to come to Canada in consideration, but if you insist I will engage to send you moreover an equal number of prisoners and allow you to name the persons. I have done everything in my power to restrain the Indians from hurting women and children who fell into their hands.

In spite of strenuous efforts to prevent it, the Indians carried off a number of women and children to their villages. Most of these were from time to time purchased from them by Col. Butler and other officers and liberated. Their temporary detention more than anything else contributed to hasten the release of Mrs. Butler and her partners in captivity. About the middle of February an Indian arrived at Niagara bearing a letter from Gen. James Clinton, who had succeeded Schuyler in command at Albany, assenting to the proposed exchange, but accusing the officers and men of the Rangers of conniving at the crimes and outrages committed by the Indians, and asserting that similar acts had been perpetrated when no Indians were present.

To this Walter Butler made a prompt and indignant reply, confidently appealing to the prisoners themselves for confirmation of his statements.

> We deny, (he said,) any cruelties to have been committed at Wyoming either by whites or Indians; so far to the contrary, that not a man, woman or child was hurt after the capitulation, or a woman or child before it, or taken into captivity. Though should you call it inhumanity, the killing men in arms in the field, we in that case plead guilty. The inhabitants killed at Cherry Valley do not lay at my door; my conscience acquits me. If any are guilty (as accessories) it's yourselves; at least the conduct of some of your officers, first, Col. Hartley, of your forces, sent to the Indians the enclosed, being a copy of his letter charging them with crimes they never committed, and threatening them and their villages with fire and sword, and no quarters.
>
> The burning of one of their villages, then inhabited only by a few families—your friends—who imagined they might remain in peace and friendship with you, till assured, a few hours before the arrival of your troops, that they should not even receive quarter, took to the woods; and, to complete the matter, Colonel Denniston and his people appearing again in arms with Colonel Hartley, after a solemn capitulation and agreement not to bear arms during the war, and Colonel Denniston not performing a promise to release a number of soldiers belonging to Colonel Butler's corps of Rangers, then prisoners among you, were the reasons assigned by the Indians to me, after the destruction of Cherry Valley, for their not acting in the same manner as at Wyoman. They added, that being charged by their enemies with what they never had done, and threatened by them, they had determined to convince you that it was not fear which had prevented them from committing the one, and putting your threats against them in force against yourselves.

The prisoners sent back by me, or any now in our or the Indians' hands, but must declare I did everything in my power to prevent the Indians killing the prisoners, or taking women and children captive, or in any way injuring them. Colonel Stacey and several other officers of yours, when exchanged, will acquit me; and must further declare that they have received every assistance, both before and since their arrival at this post, that could be got to relieve their wants. I must beg leave, by-the-bye, to observe that I experienced no humanity, or even common justice, during my imprisonment among you.

Six full companies of Rangers were assembled at Fort Niagara in December, 1778, to receive their clothing, and they then went into winter quarters in an isolated range of log buildings, constructed under Colonel Butler's supervision during the autumn, on the west side of the river, henceforth known as the "Rangers' Barracks." The uniform selected for them was of dark green cloth, trimmed with scarlet—very similar to the present rifle uniform—with a low, flat cap, having a brass plate in front bearing the monogram "G. R.," encircled by the words "Butler's Rangers." It was intended that they should be armed with rifles, but as each man was expected to provide his own they brought with them any kind of firearm they were able to procure, and in consequence many of their arms were found to be old and nearly unserviceable. Colonel Bolton lent them a hundred "firelocks" from the magazine, but confessed that there was not a single good flint in the place.

The enormous expense and the great difficulty experienced in supplying the wants of the garrison, Rangers, and refugee loyalists had already convinced General Haldimand of the great advantage that might be derived from the establishment of a permanent settlement at Niagara. The sole credit of the project may be fairly ascribed to him. For a dozen years back the military gardens formed at Oswego and Niagara, had been noted for the size and fine quality of the vegetables produced in them, specimens of which the officers occasionally sent down to astonish their friends at Montreal and Albany. The governor knew the fertility of the soil, and believed that its cultivation might be readily extended for the maintenance of the garrison.

On the 7th October, 1778, he wrote to Col. Bolton, suggesting that the refugees might be usefully employed in tilling land near the fort. Bolton's health was poor, he disliked the place, and his first reply was not encouraging. He said:

It would require seven years to bring land under cultivation to supply the garrison. We must be cautious how we encroach on the land of the Six Nations, as we have informed them that the Great King never deprived them of an acre since 1759, when he drove the French away.

But upon more mature consideration he wrote, on the 4th March, 1779:

The gentlemen I have consulted think, both from the soil and situation, the west side of the river, (the country belonging to the Missassaugas and in the government of Canada,) by far preferable to the east and where none of those difficulties can arise, and are of opinion an opportunity now offers to make a beginning by encouraging some of the distressed loyalists lately arrived at this post for His Majesty's protection. With the little stock they have brought, the second year they might possibly support themselves and families, and the third year they might be useful to this post. From that period the increase would be considerable, so that in six or seven years such a plan would be serviceable to the government and the individuals that would undertake it.

In his letters to Butler, Haldimand constantly referred to the necessity of provisioning and protecting Niagara from attack at all hazards.

Your own knowledge of the importance of Niagara will suggest the necessity of your corps, and that people (the Indians) having a constant eye to the designs of the rebels, and in case of need of throwing yourselves into that place to join in its defence. . . The great expense and difficulty of transporting provisions to Niagara makes it desirable that cattle should be driven in, or any other articles sent in to Colonel Bolton, who would pay a reasonable price for them.

Butler was able to assure him that although the Rangers, having no other means of subsistence, generally consumed most of the captured cattle, more than a hundred had been brought in by them.

The governor also signified his thorough approval of the conduct of the Rangers, while he heartily regretted and condemned the cruelty of the Indians,

I have received Captain Butler's relation of the operations at Cherry Valley, (he wrote), the success of which would have afforded the greatest satisfaction if his endeavours to prevent the excesses to which the Indians in their fury are so apt to run had proved effectual. It is, however, very much to his credit that he gave proofs of his disapprobation of such proceedings, and I trust that you, and every officer serving with the savages, will never cease your exhortations till you shall at length convince them that such indiscriminate vengeance, taken even upon the treacherous and cruel enemy they are engaged with, is as useless and disreputable as it is contrary to the disposition and maxims of their King, in whose cause they are fighting.

But he did not fail to remind Butler that he regarded their assistance as indispensable as ever.

I am confident, (he said), no pains or trouble will be spared on your part to keep the different tribes in the humour of acting for the service of the Crown, and that every argument will be made use of by you to convince them how severely they would feel the contrary behaviour.

During the winter the Indians professed to be in great fear of an attack, Butler reported that Congress had its emissaries everywhere, and that they were using every art to draw the Indians over to their side. They actually succeeded with some of the Onondagas, and made use of them to convert others.

Scouts from Niagara were constantly sent out in every direction to guard against surprise. The main body of the Rangers were held in perpetual readiness to march wherever they might be needed, and Capt. Butler made every exertion to prepare the corps for service early in the spring.

The fatigue and hardship entailed by scouting duties alone may be judged from the return of parties out on the 2nd February, 1779.

There are two scouts ordered out upon the Ohio, towards Fort Pitt and the places, adjacent, to observe the motions of the enemy, and Lieuts. Dochstader and Johnson are sent to reside among the Indians in that quarter in order to have scouts constantly out, and to send the earliest intelligence to this place. Mr. Secord is sent to Shimong for the purpose of keeping a constant watch upon the rebels towards Wyoming, from whence I daily expect intelligence, as parties have been out that way for some time. Capt. Johnson is stationed among the Senecas, with orders to use his utmost endeavours to gain every intelligence of the enemy's designs, and have sent by express any accounts of material import as well to Capt. Aubrey at Carleton Island as to the commanding officer of this garrison.

Several parties are out towards Fort Stanwix. De Quoin's son has undertaken with a party to watch the road between Fort Stanwix and the German Flats, and to intercept, if possible, some express of the rebels, and an Indian went from this some time ago whom I have engaged to make his way to Albany to observe what preparations are going on at that place, and a party has been despatched towards the Minnesinks to observe the situation of the enemy in that quarter, and the Seneca chief has promised to have some of his young men continually out, and to forward to us an account of what discoveries they make, so it will be almost impossible for the enemy to make the smallest movement in any part but we must gain immediate notice of it.

These parties had several smart skirmishes during the winter, and brought in many prisoners. The Indians were much depressed upon learning that Hamilton, governor of Detroit, had been taken by the enemy, but they quickly recovered their spirits on the arrival of Thomas Hill, a messenger from New York, with letters and newspapers relating British successes elsewhere, and announcing that large reinforcements were expected from England.

Hamilton's disaster had endangered Detroit, and Col. Bolton was compelled to send Caldwell with fifty picked Rangers to reinforce the garrison.

In the beginning of April, Lieut. John Dochstader, with 108 Indians and a few Rangers, encountered a strong body of American riflemen near Fort Pitt and cleverly drew them into an ambush. Twenty-one were killed and nine taken, with the loss of only one Indian killed and three wounded, but Dochstader himself was badly hurt in three places.

As the spring advanced, every scout and messenger brought news of the gathering of the enemy. At Fort Pitt there was a numerous force preparing boats for some unknown purpose. A formidable army was assembling at Wyoming, and a spy returning from the Mohawk announced that he had seen 700 men in camp at Canajoharie, and that it was reported they were the vanguard of an army of 3,000 advancing from that quarter against the Indians. Six hundred men from Fort Stanwix next made a raid on Onondaga. Three Indian villages were burnt, 38 women and children captured, and a few killed.

As this tribe was already friendly to the Americans, this event only served to alienate them and exasperate the remainder of the Indians. They were fast becoming convinced that their enemies intended nothing less than their total extermination.

On learning this Col. Bolton instructed Butler to march to their assistance, and on the 2nd of May he left Niagara with 400 men, including a few Indians. He was directed to advance no further than Canadasaga, the principal village of the Senecas, and keep a sharp lookout towards Fort Pitt and Wyoming, as it was surmised that the dash upon Onondaga was a mere feint to draw him in that direction. If the Americans should attempt an advance from Fort Pitt upon Detroit, he must follow at once "to escort the general's baggage."

At the same time it was equally necessary to keep strong scouts out towards Oswego, to prevent the Oneidas from discovering the weakness of the garrison at Niagara. But being among the Indians and acting in defence of their country, it soon became evident that he must to a great extent be "governed by the old Smoky Heads or chiefs."

They were panic stricken by a false alarm that the Americans were advancing on Cayuga, and compelled Butler to hurry forward by forced marches, leaving his baggage and provisions to struggle after him on pack-horses from Irondequot Bay. Everywhere he found the Indians on the very brink of starvation; many of them were actually living on roots and leaves. Cattle and grain could scarcely be purchased at any price. Scouts confirmed the report that an overwhelming army was assembling on the Susquehanna, and said that the frontier settlements were everywhere protected by a girdle of strong stockades.

In response to the most urgent appeals to send him provisions, Haldimand could say nothing more encouraging than that Butler must attempt "some stroke to procure subsistence for the Rangers" until the fleet of "victuallers" arrived from England, adding that he must hold his ground at all hazards while there was any prospect of an invasion of the Indian country. Long before this letter could reach him, Butler had attempted to put his advice into effect.

Captain McDonnel had been ordered to rejoin his regiment, but being "a spirited, prudent officer," Butler ventured to detain and sent

him with sixty men to alarm the settlements on the Mohawk, lieutenant Thompson, with forty Rangers, accompanied by Rowland Montour and a few Indians, was detached to the Susquehanna to obtain
cattle. Lieutenant Johnson made a raid upon Schoharie and brought
off eighteen prisoners, but their presence only added to his distress, as
did the arrival of numerous recruits and refugees. One bold recruiting
officer had gone within sight of Albany and brought in twenty men
belonging to Burgoyne's army. Another actually penetrated beyond
the Hudson and enlisted seventy men.

Butler urged the Indians to plant as much corn as possible, and
every Ranger not otherwise employed was set at work to assist them
in the fields on the fertile Genessee flats. By the beginning of June his
stock of provisions was exhausted, the Rangers were living from hand
to mouth, and the starving Indians were wasting his scanty supply of
ammunition by firing at every wretched little bird they saw in the
woods. It seemed impossible to remain much longer at Canadasaga,
and Butler began to tremble lest he should fail to obtain food enough
to carry his men out of the country, leaving the inhabitants to their
horrible fate.

It is pleasing to find that even in this extremity he did not relax his
efforts to redeem the prisoners still in the hands of the Indians.

> I have procured the releasement of Mrs. Campbell, (he wrote
> on the 18th June.) I have sent her with Mr. Seacord to Niagara.
> She is much in want of clothing and other necessaries. If there
> is not a more convenient place, I told her she might stay at my
> house. I expect in a few days to get Mrs. Moore and family re-
> leased likewise. The Indians have given me seven prisoners they
> have brought in at different times. I shall send them to Niagara
> the first opportunity.

On the 3rd July a deserter came in from Wyoming bringing, as it
proved, very reliable information. He stated that when he left, Gen.
Hand was encamped there with 600 men, and Generals Sullivan and
Maxwell were daily expected with nine regiments and nine cannon.
Another army was to advance from "North River," and a third from
Fort Pitt.

> They intend to cut off the Indians as they come along, and
> then join and attack Niagara. They had 600 packhorses, and
> were to have 400 more. A great number of boats were lying in
> the river.

There could no longer be any doubt that a very serious invasion was contemplated, although it was still generally supposed that the numbers of the enemy were much exaggerated. To distract their attention as much as possible, and occupy them in the defence of their own frontiers, as well as to procure supplies, McDonnel with 60 Rangers, a few volunteers from the 8th, and 100 Indians, was sent to the west branch of the Susquehanna, while Barent Frey and Brant marched against Minnesink on the Deleware.

Meanwhile, scouting parties returning from the Mohawk discovered an encampment of troops at "Cochran's Lake," supposed to be the advance-guard of the army coming from "North River." They likewise brought the doleful news that Lieut. Henry Hare and Sergt. Newberry of the Rangers had been taken by the enemy and executed as spies. Hare had been recognized while "viewing the stores as they passed up the river," and was hanged on a gallows, erected, with a refinement of cruelty, in front of his own house.

Their comrades were bitterly exasperated, and made fierce threats of retaliation in like manner.

By the 19th July every expedient that ingenuity and experience could suggest for the maintenance of the remainder of his battalion at Canadasaga had been exhausted. Lieut. Thompson wrote from Tioga that he had been unable to procure any cattle, and must either return or starve. The Indians were continually begging for food, which it was not in his power to supply. The small stock of provisions sent by Bolton from Niagara had long since been consumed, although great care had been taken "to make it go as far as possible, and the men only allowed as much as was barely sufficient to keep them alive, which has brought actual sickness on some and endangered the lives of the whole."

> To add to all this, (Butler continued), there is not the same opportunity of driving cattle from the enemy's frontier as there was the preceding summer. Many of the settlements were then broken, and such as remain are secured by a chain of forts, which the enemy maintain at small distances all along their frontier, and had I a prospect of taking any of them I could not march out against them with a sufficient body for want of provisions.

Genessee Falls, two days' march from Canadasaga, was selected as a suitable place for an encampment, where the Rangers could be supplied with provisions by boats from Niagara, and the abundance of fish in the river would afford a welcome change of diet to men who had been living, for many weeks, on stale salt meat imported from Ireland.

> Should we be wanted at Oswego, (Butler explained), it will be the most convenient place for us to move from to it. Should our services be required towards Fort Pitt, Detroit, or Venango, there is no place can be at all so centrical for either of those places. In justice to the people under my command I could no longer delay it, as they were suffering everything that disease and hunger could inflict, and had they remained in this situation much longer would have been entirely unfit for service.

He himself still remained at Canadasaga to sustain the spirits of the Indians, and vigilant officers were stationed in all their outlying villages with instructions to keep scouts out in every direction.

While Butler was so employed both the parties he had sent out against the frontiers had struck damaging blows, after a "very fatiguing and tedious march over mountains and through woods almost impenetrable," McDonnel gained the west branch of the Susquehanna. On the 27th July he marched all night and at daybreak came in sight of Fort Freeland, the frontier post. Before noon the garrison capitulated, after having two men killed. Thirty-one prisoners were taken, including a commissioner of the county. Of the besiegers only John Montour, who led a party of the Indians, was wounded, while scalping a man under the walls. Two hours later the Rangers were unexpectedly attacked by a party of seventy or eighty men from a neighbouring fort, who, having heard the firing, had advanced to the relief of Fort Freeland.

The Indians had dispersed in search of cattle and allowed them to approach unperceived until within gunshot. McDonnel hastily formed his men and engaged them in front until the Indians assembled and took the enemy in the flank, when they were quickly routed, leaving three captains and thirty men dead on the field. McDonnel said that very few would have escaped if their flight had not been favoured by thick underwood. He lost only one Indian killed and another wounded. After this skirmish he attempted to induce the Indians to follow up their success, but "they were glutted with plunder" and insisted on retreating a few miles to enjoy themselves overnight,

In the morning he returned with 100 men and destroyed five forts and thirty miles of settled country, advancing within a short distance of Shamokin. Eighty women and children were taken during the day and released uninjured. A hundred cattle were driven off, but half of them were subsequently stolen by the Indians. On the 5th of August McDonnel was again at Tioga, awaiting the approach of the enemy from Wyoming.

Brant and Frey had a very similar experience. They destroyed several small forts or stockades and many other buildings at Minnesink, with little opposition. On their retreat they were pursued by a much superior force of militia, which outmarched them and formed an ambush at the Lackawaxen ford. Quickly recovering from his surprise. Brant quietly led a party of Indians around a hill and suddenly attacked his assailants in the rear. They dispersed and were remorselessly slaughtered in their flight. More than a hundred were killed, and but one taken prisoner.

Tidings of these disasters, accompanied by urgent appeals for assistance, reached General Sullivan at Wyoming on the 29th July, but he firmly refused to be turned aside from his main purpose. He said in reply;

> Nothing could afford me more pleasure than to relieve the distressed, or to have it in my power to add to the safety of your settlement, but should I comply with the requisition made by you it would effectually answer the intention of the enemy and destroy the grand object of this expedition.

Immediately after the return of his detachments, Butler despatched Lieut. Lottridge with a small party to bring off some of the Oneidas, who had stated their wish to desert the enemy, and Lieut. Daniel Servos, with a larger one, to alarm the German Flats. He had been informed that the Americans were damming the outlet of Otsego or Cochran's Lake, with the object of raising the water in the stream leading into the Susquehanna sufficiently to float their boats, and the indefatigable Brant went in that direction to observe their movements. He returned with some prisoners, but limping from an ugly wound in the foot. By that time Sullivan's advance-guard had arrived at Tioga, where it was evidently waiting for the junction of the division from Otsego Lake.

The force intended for the invasion of the Indian territory had been organized in three divisions by Washington's advice, in the expectation that their converging movements would "distract and terrify" their opponents. The largest, which had gradually assembled at

Wyoming, consisted of 3,500 veteran soldiers from the Eastern States, besides 500 boatman and drivers. Clinton's division, composed chiefly of New York troops, numbered nearly 2,000. At the same time 500 men from Fort Pitt were directed to ascend the Alleghany and destroy the Seneca villages near that river.

General Sullivan, who was selected for the chief command, was a striking type of a class of shrewd, pushing, self-reliant men, of humble origin, which the Revolution had brought to the front. Beginning life as a stable-boy, he became successively a hostler, a tavern-keeper, a lawyer, a member of the Assembly, a delegate in Congress, and last of all a general in the Continental army.

> The immediate objects, (Washington informed him), are the total destruction and devastation of their settlements, and the capture of as many prisoners, of every age and sex, as possible. It will be essential to ruin their crops now in the ground and prevent them planting more. Parties should be detached to lay waste all the settlements around, with instructions to do it in the most effectual manner, that the country not be merely *over-run*, but *destroyed*.
>
> After you have very thoroughly completed the destruction of their settlements, if the Indians should show a disposition for peace I would have you encourage it, on condition that they will give some decisive evidence of their sincerity by delivering up some of the principal instigators of their past hostility into our hands; Butler, Brant, the most mischievous of the Tories that have joined them, or any others they may have in their power that we are interested to get in ours. They may possibly be engaged by address, secrecy, and stratagem to surprise the garrison at Niagara and the shipping upon the lakes, and put them in our possession.

Sullivan completed his preparations with notable deliberation and forethought, heedless of the clamour of the inhabitants for greater haste. Hundreds of boats and wagons were employed for six weeks in accumulating provisions and stores at Wyoming, where their brigades were assembled in June and carefully trained for bush-fighting. Thirty Oneidas, headed by their spiritual adviser, Kirkland, were engaged as scouts and guides.

On the last day of July he began his march from that place, with eleven regiments of infantry and rifles, and one of artillery, besides the

Wyoming militia; driving with him 800 cattle and 1200 pack-horses, and attended by 120 boats on the river, conveying his heavy baggage and nine field guns.

This force, as Butler observed, was composed of "some of the best Continental troops, commanded by the most active rebel generals, and not a regiment of militia among the whole." On the 11th August it arrived at Tioga Point and encamped between the rivers, where a strong stockade was built. The Rangers were immediately recalled to Canadasaga where Butler had assembled 300 Indians, and the whole advanced to meet the enemy. On the 13th, Sullivan with his entire division made a night march to surprise Chemung, a village of thirty houses. Their approach was discovered and the place deserted.

As they were passing through a narrow defile the invaders were attacked by Rowland Montour with forty Indians, and thrown into much confusion. Montour held his ground until nearly surrounded, when he retired with the loss of one man killed. The Americans lost twenty-one in killed or wounded, and returned to Tioga, after destroying some houses and cornfields. Butler halted at Chuckmet, fourteen miles from their camp, sending forward parties daily to reconnoitre and alarm their outposts. His scouts killed a few stragglers and drove off some horses, but failed to take a prisoner as he desired.

On the 19th Sullivan was joined by Clinton's brigade of five regiments, which had floated leisurely down the Tioga upon breaking the dam they had built. His army must then have numbered quite 6000. Leaving a strong garrison at Tioga, he deliberately resumed his advance, warily feeling every step with swarms of riflemen in front and on the flanks, and cutting a wide road through the woods for the passage of his artillery and packhorses.

Panic-stricken by the appearance of such an overwhelming army, a majority of the Indians thought only of removing their families and moveable property to a place of safety. The number of warriors that joined Butler never exceeded 300, although he had expected 1000. The Delewares had promised 200 and only sent 30. He had less than 300 Rangers and only 14 men of the 8th. There was no exaggeration when he said that the enemy were coming with as many thousands as he had hundreds. He kept up an appearance of confidence, however, and attempted to reassure the Indians by telling them he would defeat the invaders with the Rangers alone, assisted by their brethren under Brant.

Unfortunately, runners then came from the Seneca villages on the

Alleghany to announce that their country was invaded by a large force from Pittsburgh. On this, Butler tried to persuade the Indians to retire to some more advantageous position, leaving small parties among the hills to harass the Americans on their advance, but the Delewares had pointed out the spot where they ought to meet the enemy, and the others were obstinately bent upon following their advice.

Having sent away his baggage in charge of the sick, Butler accordingly marched forward and took possession of the ground indicated to him, on the 27th of August.

It was a ridge of about half-a-mile in length, to the right of which lay a large plain extending to the river and terminating in a narrow pass near our encampment, so that, having possession of the heights, we would have had greatly the advantage should the enemy direct their march that way. On our left was a steep mountain, and a large creek in our front at a little distance.

A rough breastwork was formed of logs, which they attempted to mask with freshly cut boughs. In some places shallow rifle-pits were dug, and a log building was occupied and loop-holed for musketry. McDonnel with sixty Rangers and Brant with thirty "whites and Indians" occupied the right of this position, Captain Butler with the remainder of the Rangers and the party of the 8th held the centre, while the main body of the Indians, commanded by Sangerachta, was posted on the left, at the foot of the mountain. At sunset they were informed that the enemy was still encamped below Chemung, and they retired for the night to their own camp, about a mile distant. Next day the position was again occupied from sunrise until dark, without any appearance of the Americans. But Sullivan's scouts had heard the noise of their axes in the day and seen the glare of their campfires at night.

Neither officers nor men of the Rangers had a blanket or tent to cover them, and since their arrival at Chuckmet, two weeks before, they had neither meat, flour, nor salt, but had been subsisting entirely upon a daily allowance of seven ears of green corn, which they had scarcely found time to cook.

On the 29th, at daybreak, they resumed possession of their lines "which," Butler said, "some officious fellows among the Indians altered and turned the left wing along the mountain, quite the contrary way from its original situation, which was in a great measure the cause of our defeat, as it gave the enemy room to outflank us on that wing without opposition."

Here they remained exposed to the full glare of the sun until two o'clock, when a number of riflemen appeared in the skirt of the woods. The plain between them and the breastwork was covered with tall grass rising nearly as high as a man's head. The affair at Chemung had made the Americans more than usually cautious, and before advancing into the plain some of their scouts climbed trees, from which they discovered this entrenchment and saw a number of Indians, brightly painted with vermillion, lying on the ground behind it. They at once commenced a brisk fire while their artillery was being brought forward, and a brigade of light infantry detached around the hill to turn the Rangers' position and gain the defile in the rear.

When the skirmish had lasted for half an hour, with trifling loss on either side, Butler began to suspect the enemy's purpose and urged the Indians to commence their retreat. His advice was warmly seconded by Brant and the Cayuga chief, who had come together from the opposite flank to point out the danger of remaining any longer where they were. One of the most powerful reasons for an immediate retreat was the wretched physical condition of the Rangers, who were horribly enfeebled by exposure and the poorness of their food, and at the very moment the action began three officers and several men were struck down by the ague.

But the majority of the Indians were still obstinately bent on holding their ground, and would pay no attention to their arguments. By that time the Americans had got six guns and coehorns in position and opened "an elegant cannonade," firing shells, round and grape shot, and iron spikes upon the main body of the Indians. This had an immediate and demoralizing effect. The sight of the shells bursting in their rear convinced them that they were already surrounded, and they sprang to their feet and ran away at full speed.

The Rangers and Brant's party being thus deserted, retired as rapidly as possible to the hill, which they found already occupied by the enemy's riflemen, with whom they kept up a running fight for nearly a mile, when they were obliged to disperse in every direction—some fording the river, others escaping along the wooded summit of the hill. Butler himself narrowly avoided capture. Many of the Indians never halted in their flight till they reached their respective villages, but the Rangers reassembled before dark at Nanticoketown, five miles distant, and continued their retreat until they overtook their baggage.

Their actual loss had been miraculously small—only five men were killed or missing, and three wounded. The Indians reported a loss of five killed and nine wounded. Sullivan acknowledged a loss of forty-two killed and wounded among his regular troops, and at least one of his Oneida scouts was killed besides.

His victorious troops amused themselves by scalping the dead, and in two cases actually skinned the bodies of Indians from the hips downward, to make boot tops or leggings.

Next day Sullivan sent back all unnecessary baggage and some of his heaviest cannon to Tioga and resumed his advance in the same deliberate and cautious but resistless manner, laying waste the scattered villages, cornfields and orchards he passed, in the most thorough-going fashion imaginable. Judge Jones relates that he often heard Butler compare his march to "driving a wedge into a stick of wood; nothing stopped or disturbed its motion." Indian runners constantly watched his progress from the hill-tops, and warned their tribesmen of his approach, so that he found their houses always deserted and empty.

Half of Butler's men were sick and absolutely unfit for duty, and he fell back to Canadasaga, sending to the mouth of the Genessee for removal to Niagara. The mass of the Indians were thoroughly dispirited, and even the influence and example of Brant and Sangerachta, who behaved throughout with admirable courage and firmness, failed to rally many of them to his support. The Cayugas sent an Oneida to beg for mercy for their tribe, but Sullivan haughtily replied that Congress had "instructed him totally to extirpate the unfriendly nations of Indians, to subdue their country, destroy their crops, and drive them to seek habitations where they would be less troublesome."

Captain Butler continued to watch Sullivan's motions with a few picked Rangers and some Indians that were kept together by the tireless exertions of Brant and Rowland Montour. On the 7th Sept. the American army took possession of Canadasaga, but the Indians by that time had slightly recovered their spirits, and agreed to collect all their forces and fight them once more before they could reach Genessee. Many of the Rangers who had been disabled by the ague had also recovered sufficiently to bear arms again, and cheerfully returned to join their comrades. Bolton, who was seriously alarmed for the safety of his post, sent the light company of the 8th to Butler's assistance, followed by that of the 34th immediately on its arrival from Carleton Island.

On the 12th Butler marched from Canawagoras with 400 Rangers and Indians, and early next morning formed an ambush upon the path by which the enemy was advancing. By the Indians' request the Rangers were mingled with them to keep up their courage, and for some hours the entire party lay concealed among dense thickets in close vicinity to Sullivan's vanguard, which was busily engaged in felling trees and building a bridge over a morass at the head of Lake Conesus, with the intention of allowing part of his army to pass across, and attacking it in such a way as to prevent the remainder from coming to its support. They were then startled by a sudden burst of musketry on the right, and the Indians, crying out they were surrounded, ran hastily in that direction.

When Butler reached the spot he found that an American scout of thirty men, in rambling through the woods, had stumbled into the midst of the Rangers and Indians on that flank. Twenty-two of them were killed by a single volley, and Lieut. Boyd and a private taken prisoner. Boyd told him that their army still numbered 5,000, including 1,500 riflemen, that they had only a month's provisions when they began their march, and that they did not intend to advance beyond Genessee. Butler immediately retired across the Genessee, and the next morning the American army appeared on the opposite bank.

All the Indians except forty at once deserted him, and he abandoned the place. Before night he arrived at Buffalo Creek, on his way to Niagara. He then learned that Caldwell's company had been ordered down from Detroit, and that Sir John Johnson, with 380 men, was daily expected at Carleton Island, with instructions to proceed to his support by way of Oswego. Five thousand famishing Indians had taken refuge at Niagara. Caldwell, with a small party, was sent to pursue Sullivan, who was reported to be already retiring. He found that the fort, at Tioga had been abandoned and burnt, and there were unquestionable signs that the American army had retreated with much haste. Its line of march was strewed with the bodies of packhorses that had been shot as they gave out, and several hundred cattle and horses were running wild in the woods about Tioga. Caldwell advanced sixteen miles further, but his Indians refused to go to Wyoming as he desired, and compelled him to return to Niagara.

Sullivan reported that he had destroyed forty Indian villages; but several others had escaped his notice, besides a number of extensive cornfields near Genessee. But he had not succeeded in taking half-a-dozen prisoners during the whole expedition, although this had been indicated as one of its principal objects. In spite of his precautions to prevent it, some of his soldiers were guilty of acts of revolting cruelty. One party killed a lame squaw in cold blood; another shut a helpless man and woman in a cabin which they then set on fire and left them to perish miserably. In many respects his campaign was practically a failure. One of his officers truthfully remarked in his journal, " The nests are destroyed but the birds are still on the wing." His severity only served to exasperate the Indians and render them more impatient of restraint in the future.

During Caldwell's absence Butler was directed to join Sir John Johnson at Sodus Bay with the remainder of the Rangers, General Haldimand took that opportunity to convey to him the gratifying information that;

> His Majesty has been made acquainted with your services, he has approved of them, and I hope the events of this campaign will recommend you still more to his Royal favour.

Many of the Rangers being sick and others detached, the number of effective men at his disposal did not exceed 200. The expedition proved an utter failure. On the 4th October, Sir John Johnson sailed from Carleton Island for Sodus, but was driven into Niagara next day by a terrific gale. Butler was still there, and several days were consumed in lengthy councils with the Indians. On the 10th, the troops were embarked in three sailing vessels, and Brant with some Indians marched overland to the Three Rivers, where he proposed to await their arrival. The Oneida village was selected as the first point of attack.

On the 15th, Johnson and Butler arrived at Oswego, where they remained until the 20th, when the camp was alarmed by a sentry firing at a prowling Indian. A scout from the Rangers went out and captured three Oneidas, who confessed that their tribe had been warned of their danger by a Cayuga from Niagara, and had sent them to watch their motions. All prospect of taking them by surprise being clearly at an end, Johnson returned to Carleton Island and sent the Rangers into winter quarters at Niagara, where they arrived with their clothing torn to rags by hard service.

Haldimand was so profoundly discouraged by the events of the summer that he warned Lord G. Germain that, if he expected to preserve the "upper country and fur trade," a body of 1000 or 1500 men, with the necessary supply of provisions, must be employed for that service alone, as soon as the river became navigable in the spring. In the same letter (13th Sept., 1779,) he requested permission to carry on this scheme of forming settlements near the principal forts:

I have for many years regretted that measures were not adopted such as to prevent the safety of those posts depending upon supplies from home, so very distant, the transportation so extremely precarious, and attended with so heavy an expense to government; all of which might be obviated, the troops infinitely better provided, and the different posts be in perfect security by raising grain and all kinds of stock at Detroit, which, from its centrical situation, could very well supply both Detroit and Machilimakinac.

The same plan is very practicable at Niagara, and there is nothing wanting but a beginning. It will be necessarily attended with some expense the first two or three years, but would even in as many more amply repay it. In these times nothing can be vigorously undertaken, but should this unfortunate war terminate, it should immediately be carried into execution, and in such case I should be happy to receive your lordship's approbation of, and commands to undertake, what I am convinced would produce the most salutary effects for His Majesty's interests in those parts.

As the Indian villages were no longer in existence to serve even as a temporary base of supplies for the Rangers, the character of their operations necessarily changed. Their marches became very much lengthened, and the hardships and perils attending their expeditions were greatly increased. The difficulty of obtaining supplies seriously hampered their movements, and a drove of cattle was the most precious spoil they could seize. The size of their parties was generally diminished and as many of them as possible were mounted, and they drove with them a few cattle, each of which had a bag of flour and another of salt tied on its back. The officer in command kept a journal, in which the events of the expedition were more or less fully noted. Some of these have been preserved, but it is certain that all record of many stirring incidents of these adventurous journeys perished with the actors, and only a bare outline now remains in most cases.

Each officer had written instructions prescribing his route, and usually directing him;

. . . . to destroy any magazines or granaries which afford supplies to the rebels, as well as to kill or take any of them who are enemies or in arms, shewing humanity to women, children or aged persons, and endeavouring to obtain all intelligence in your power of the state of affairs, or to bring off any persons well affected to His Majesty's service.

Congress had fully acknowledged the importance of their operations in the past, by withdrawing a division of 5,000 of its best troops from the principal seat of war for an entire year, in the hope of crushing them. The annoyance and damage occasioned by the system of guerrilla warfare, now inaugurated, was indescribably harassing to the enemy, and there can be no doubt that the presence of the Rangers with the Indians was the means of preserving many lives.

Patrick Campbell, late a captain in the 42nd, visited both Niagara and the Mohawk valley in 1791, when the memory of these events was still fresh in the mind; of everybody. He writes of the exploits of the Rangers with undisguised enthusiasm.

> This chosen corps—this band of brothers—was rarely worsted in any skirmish or action, though often obliged to retire and betake themselves to the wilderness when a superior force came against them. Sir John's corps and Butler's Rangers were very distressing to the back settlers, their advances and retreats were equally sudden and astonishing, and to this day the Americans say they might have as easily, found out a parcel of wolves in the woods as them if they once entered it; that the first notice they had of their approach was them in sight, and of their retreat their being out of reach .... I have known many of them, both officers and soldiers, and the account they gave of the fatigue and suffering they underwent is hard credible, were it not confirmed by one and all of them.

Equally creditable is the testimony of the traveller Long, another contemporary.

> During the American war, (he remarks), the best Loyalist troops were collected from the Mohawk, and it was agreed on all hands that for steadiness, bravery, and allegiance they were not to be excelled.

Late in the autumn of 1779, Guy Johnson arrived at Niagara and assumed control of the Indian department. Butler continued to act as his deputy. The Cayugas and Delewares, dispirited by their misfortunes, showed unmistakable signs of defection. They blamed Butler for permitting the destruction of their villages, and even threatened to deliver him into the hands of the Americans if he ventured among them again. But want soon compelled them to seek relief at Niagara, and their resentment gradually passed away when they found that their enemies were determined to show them no mercy.

Had Sullivan acted with more prudence and less severity, (Bolton observed in May, 1780), I am satisfied we should not have had one-third of the Six Nations in our interest at the present time.

The Wyandots and Shawanese in the immediate vicinity of Fort Pitt actually sued for terms, and Col. Brodhead, who commanded there, promised them protection on the conditions that they would bring him "as many scalps and prisoners from the English and their allies" as they had formerly taken from the Americans, and that they would join him "in every case against the enemies of America."

The remarkable severity of the winter even prevented scouting parties from going out until late in February. The river at Niagara was frozen over for two months at a stretch, and in the gorges of the Alleghanies the snow lay in many places eight and ten feet deep. The sufferings of the Indians were frightful, and many perished from cold and hunger. More than 2,600 wore encamped in frail *wigwams* around Fort Niagara, and the remainder sought shelter in the villages that had escaped destruction.

Recruiting officers from the Rangers lay concealed among the settlements throughout the winter, and succeeded, with little difficulty, in enlisting a sufficient number of men to complete the battalion to its full strength. Butler was promoted to the rank and pay of a Provincial Lieutenant-Colonel, but Gen. Haldimand declined to approve of the appointment of a Major and Adjutant for the corps, as he desired. The governor took occasion to say in respect to this;

Rangers are in general separated, and the nature of their service little requires the forms of parade or the manoeuvres practised in the field. It is the duty, and I am persuaded will be the pleasure, of every captain to perfect his company in dispersing and forming expeditiously, priming and loading carefully, and levelling well. These, with personal activity and alertness, are all the qualities that are effective or can be wished for in a Ranger.

They were accordingly carefully exercised in these particulars, and in the management of two light field-guns, called grasshoppers.

Early in the spring of 1780, one company was sent to Detroit and another to Caneton Island, to act as scouts for those garrisons.

The first blow was struck by Sir John Johnson, who marched secretly from Crown Point on the 9th May, with 300 soldiers and Indians. On the 21st he appeared among the settlements near Johnson Hall, having advanced through the wilderness without being discovered. He took a few prisoners and devastated a long stretch of country with slight opposition. He was joined by 143 loyalists who were expecting his arrival, and retired without loss, although pursued by the governor of the State with a thousand men.

Pittsburg was blockaded by Lieut. Dochstader and Fort Stanwix by Brant and Capt. Nelles, and some small parties cut off at both places.

In June, McDonnel with sixty Rangers, accompanied by 100 Indians under Capt. John Johnson, marched against the Oneida villages. The indecision of the Indians prevented him from accomplishing anything he had intended. A few Oneidas joined his party and the remainder promised to follow. McDonnel was struck down by an ague fit which continued for ten days, and his men were forced to tie him upon his horse during the return march. In July, 300 Indians, chiefly Onondagas and Tuscaroras, "hitherto in the rebel interest," actually arrived at Niagara.

Brant and Clement with 300 men marched immediately against the recalcitrant Oneidas. They found their principal village entirely deserted, and burned the fort built for its protection. On approaching Fort Stanwix they discovered the Oneidas encamped under the walls. After a short parley about a hundred of them agreed to join Brant, and the remainder ran for shelter to the fort, which they reached with the exception of two that were shot dead in their flight.

After blockading the place closely for some days Brant retreated a short distance to remove suspicion, and then, making a long circuit, advanced by forced marches upon Claes' Barrack, where he appeared on the morning of the 2nd August. He detached David Karacanty with the greater part of the Indians against Fort Plank, but the garrison had already taken the alarm. Two small forts were abandoned on his approach and destroyed, with several mills and many other buildings, containing great quantities of grain.

Fifty prisoners were captured, besides many women and children who were at once released. Five hundred horses and cattle were driven off. Before the inhabitants could recover from their surprise, Brant had vanished, and subdividing his force into five parties he sent them by as many different routes against Schoharie, Cherry Valley, and the German Flats, where they took many more prisoners and created great alarm. On their arrival at Niagara the Oneidas professed much contrition for their past conduct and surrendered a flag and one of eleven officer's commissions distributed among them by the Americans.

At the same time many other parties were similarly engaged on the Susquehanna and Ohio. So greatly harassed were the frontiers of Pennsylvania that the Executive Council of the State determined to offer a reward for prisoners and scalps, a step which had been strongly recommended from several quarters. In April, 1780, President Reed definitely announced their decision to the lieutenants of the border counties and other military officers. To Colonel Hunter he wrote:

> The council would and do for the purpose authorize you to offer the following premiums; For every male prisoner, white or Indian, if the former is acting with the latter, $1500, and $1000 for every Indian scalp. The proof must be left to your own discretion, not doubting your care to prevent imposition. We do not recollect one single instance of recovering a single captive or plunder, killing or taking any of the enemy, though so many pursuits have been attempted.

Reed informed Colonel Brodhead that;

> . . . .after many consultations and much deliberation, we have concluded to offer a reward for scalps, and we hope it will prove an incentive for young fellows of the country and others to turn out against the Indians.

In reply Brodhead warned the Council that;

> . . . . the Delewares act with our scouts, and I have great reason to believe a considerable number will join me upon the first capital enterprise I can undertake. I fear it (the reward) may be construed into a license to take off the scalps of some of our friendly Delewares, and so produce a general Indian war.

In a subsequent letter he lamented that the reward had not been extended to;

> . . . .officers, soldiers, and friendly Indians, because I conceive it would have been a sure method to save the friendly Indians and destroy some of the hostile ones, and perhaps involve the Indians in a war against one another.

Several companies of Rangers armed, accoutred, and often painted like Indians, were soon formed, and numerous small forts and block-houses built for their protection. But even these energetic measures failed to save their border settlements from destruction. Every day brought its lamentable tale of bloodshed and ruin. One officer wrote:

The inhabitants have been flying for a week past. I believe there will not be a family in Northumberland town tomorrow morning. We ought to have Niagara, cost what it will.

The lieutenant of Bedford County said: "A number of our militia companies are entirely broke up." Their fears, he added, had recently been aggravated by "a most alarming stroke," which had been ex-ecuted by Lieutenant Dochstader on the 16th July. With an inconsid-erable party of Indians he had surprised a blockhouse in Woodcock Valley, occupied by a captain and eleven of the newly formed Rangers. Unhappily, the country was alarmed, and, being warmly pursued, the Indians insisted on putting ten of the prisoners to death to ensure their own escape.

In various secluded valleys many quiet loyalists still lived undis-turbed upon their farms, from whom the Rangers frequently received shelter and supplies. Such an isolated community existed at this time in the almost inaccessible Catawisse Valley, on a branch of the Susque-hanna above Wyoming, walled in by towering hills. Complaints were lodged against the inhabitants, that "they have lived peaceably in the most dangerous times, negroes and other suspected strangers being frequently seen amongst them. During every incursion the enemy have made into this country. all the disaffected families fly there for protection, whilst the well-affected are obliged to evacuate the coun-try or shut themselves in garrison."

The destruction of this settlement was decreed, and Colonel Cairns, the lieutenant of the county, marched to accomplish it with a company of volunteers. It was preserved for the time by the acciden-tal appearance of Lieut. Wm. Johnston and Rowland Montour with forty Rangers and Indians. This party had invested Fort Rice, "at the head of Chilloskewagie," on the 5th September, where they spent a day in destroying the surrounding settlement. Then marching against Fort Jenkins, at Wyoming, they destroyed it, and detached ten men to conduct the prisoners and captured cattle to Niagara. Johnston and Montour, with the remainder, turned westward, and, on the 10th, un-expectedly discovered Cairns with 41 men advancing upon Catawisse.

Concealing themselves, they obtained the advantage of the first fire, and in an instant routed his entire party, killing the colonel and fifteen others, and taking three prisoners. Only one Indian was killed at the time, but Rowland Montour, long known as "a brave and active chief," received a wound in the arm from which he died a week later.

Early in the course of the same month Haldimand determined to send two larger expeditions against the frontiers of New York. Each of these was to consist of about 600 men, and they wore to advance simultaneously; one from Crown Point towards Albany and the other from Oswego upon the Mohawk River. The objects of these movements, he explained, were "to divide the strength that may be brought against Sir H. Clinton, to favour any operations his present situation may enable him to carry out, as well as to destroy the enemy's supplies from the late plentiful harvest and to give His Majesty's loyal subjects an opportunity of retiring to this province," and at the same time to force the remaining Oneidas "to obedience or to cut them off" Sir John Johnson was sent to Oswego with 150 of his own regiment, and Butler was directed to join him with 140 of the 8th, 80 of the 34th, and 200 Rangers, taking with him a grasshopper and two royals from Niagara.

> I would by no means, (the governor added in a letter to Bolton), have you send a single man who is not a good marcher and capable of bearing fatigue. The same must be observed in your choice of officers, without paying attention to the rosters, as success will entirely depend upon your despatch and vigour; those whose personal abilities are not equal to these efforts would rather weaken than give strength to the detachment, for with every man that falls out one or two must be left behind . . . .The chief danger of a discovery is from disaffected Indians from Carleton Island or Niagara, I hope Joseph (Brant) is returned, as I would by all means have him employed in this service . . . .The troops are to be provided with a blanket, leggings, and a pair of *moccasins*.

His letter found the small garrison of Niagara more than usually weakened by disease. Bolton averred that he had never before known so many men to be sick at once. The detachments were detailed with much difficulty in consequence, and Butler embarked on the 24th September, taking with him every Ranger that could be of the slightest service, including some convalescents and a number of Indians collected in extreme haste. Contrary winds prevented their vessels from arriving at Oswego until the 1st October. They began their march next day, conveying their artillery and baggage in boats as far as Onondaga, where the boats and a quantity of provisions were concealed. The guns were then placed upon rude sleds hastily constructed on the spot, and ten days' provisions were served out to each man.

On the 8th they arrived at Old Oneida where they were rejoined by a scouting party bringing some prisoners from the German Flats, who stated that two Oneidas had passed through some days before on their way from Niagara to Albany spreading the news that Butler had gone on an expedition with a large party. The day following one of their own Oneidas deserted. On the 12th another scout returned with more prisoners, who confirmed the former accounts, but said that the inhabitants had no suspicion that they were so near. By this time, their provisions were almost exhausted, and another party was sent forward to a Scotch settlement at Schoharie to obtain a supply. Two Cayugas then deserted, and it was with great difficulty that the remainder of the Indians were prevented from following their example, as they were intimidated by a report that 2,000 of the enemy had already collected to meet them.

On the 15th, the foraging party returned with eleven cattle, which were instantly slaughtered and distributed among the hungry soldiers. They then pushed on as rapidly as possible, and just before daybreak, on the 17th, passed the fort at the head of the Schoharie. The roar of three alarm-guns announced that they had been discovered, and orders were given to set fire to every building as they went along. Heralded by lurid flames and rolling clouds of smoke they swept onward to the middle fort, which they hoped to take. The Rangers and Indians surrounded this work and fired smartly at the embrasures and; loopholes until the royals could be brought forward to make a breach.

A few rounds convinced them that these light guns would make no impression upon the stout logs of the fort, and Capt. Andrew Thompson of the Rangers was sent to summon the garrison. He was deliberately fired at three times by a noted marksman, but returned unhurt. The march was then resumed, torch in hand, along the road leading down the west bank of Schoharie Kill to the Mohawk. A scout sent from below to observe their motions was overtaken and three men killed or captured. The royals had been slung across a horse for convenience of transport—but finding they were a great encumbrance they were taken off and buried in a swamp.

The roads were so bad that even the light three-pounder fieldpieces were dragged forward with much labour. When they approached the river, Capt. Thompson and Brant with 150 Rangers and Indians were sent across the creek to destroy the settlement around Fort Hunter, on the opposite bank, which they quickly accomplished and rejoined the main body soon after they had reached the Mohawk. Thence they swiftly advanced up the river, laying waste the entire country on both sides until midnight, when they halted at the narrow pass called "The Nose." They had then been under arms for full twenty-four hours, spent in almost continuous exertion, and were utterly overcome by fatigue. During the night two men who had deserted from Fort Stanwix in the spring and enlisted in Johnson's regiment, again deserted and informed Colonel Brown, who commanded at Stone Arabia, of the weakness of the party on that side of the river.

Brown determined to attack it at daybreak with 360 men in the hope of crushing it before it could be reinforced. However, Johnson had by that time crossed the river with nearly his whole force, leaving only a few light troops on the other side, and was advancing upon Stone Arabia in the midst of a dense fog. A few horsemen were seen in front viewing their numbers, who then disappeared. Brown's force was next discovered posted in a wood behind a log fence, having a narrow lane and wide open field in front. A party of Indians began the attack, but were soon driven back. Johnson sent forward small parties of the Rangers, 8th, and 34th to their support and a brisk skirmish commenced.

While the attention of the Americans was thus occupied in front, Brant with a body of Indians made a circuit through the woods to turn their right flank, while McDonnell led the Rangers in the opposite direction to gain their left. Johnson then charged their position with the remainder of the 8th and 34th, leaping over the fence and driving them out of the woods. Colonel Brown was killed with nearly 100 of his men, according to Johnson's account, but the Americans only admitted a loss of forty or forty-five in all. A private of the 8th and three Indians were killed, three Rangers were wounded, and Brant received a painful flesh wound in the foot, which disabled him from marching.

In company with McDonnell he was particularly commended by Johnson for courage and activity on this occasion. Letters found in Colonel Brown's pocket revealed the fact that General Van Rensselaer, with 600 militia and three guns, in pursuit of them, had arrived at

Fort Hunter the night before, and firing had not yet ceased when his advance guard appeared on the other bank of the river. His force had by this time increased to 1500, including two regiments of Continentals and nearly a hundred Oneida Indians, and he was accompanied by Governor Clinton himself. When they became aware of Brown's disastrous defeat they halted in dismay, and Johnson continued his march through Stone Arabia, burning everything in his track.

Three miles further on the road was blocked by a fort which compelled him to march through the fields, and at the Fort Hendricks' ford he was forced to make a second detour to avoid the fire of several fortified houses. Upon regaining the high road at sunset he found that Van Rensselaer had crossed the river and had securely posted his entire force in the houses and orchards in front. Sending a strong party to seize a hill overlooking and commanding the road Johnson immediately attacked this position with the remainder and drove them across a field. The Americans reformed under the guns of the fort, and Johnson's Indians, discovering that they were greatly outnumbered, were seized by a panic and rode through the ford in frantic haste to escape.

Encouraged by their headlong flight the Americans advanced on the left, creeping silently forward in the growing darkness under cover of the trees and fences, and began a very hot fire at close quarters. The detachment of the 34th and part of Johnson's regiment gave way and were pursued by the enemy with loud cheers. A single, well-aimed discharge of grape, and a volley of musketry from the remainder of the line drove them back and totally silenced their fire. Van Rensselaer's men were so much shaken by this final repulse that he retreated three miles and permitted Johnson to pass the ford, thus laid open to him, without the slightest molestation. The Indians led the way into the woods, but they dared not halt for an instant, although almost fainting with fatigue and lack of sleep. In the darkness they lost their way and separated into several parties.

One of these, under Captain Parke of the 8th, strayed off in the direction of Fort Herkimer, at the German Flats, where they arrived next morning and discovered sixty of the enemy marching to join Van Rensselaer. Uncertain of their numbers Parke hastily ordered his men to take to the woods and avoid a collision. But the stout-hearted McDonnell then came up with a few Rangers. He boldly charged the enemy without hesitation, killing ten, taking two prisoners and driving the rest into the fort without having a single man hurt. Meanwhile Parke had gone on rapidly. McDonnell missed his trail and did not succeed in rejoining Johnson until the second day after, when the entire force was reunited with the exception of about forty men. They continued their retreat with all possible speed in their exhausted state, until they reached the Oneida Village. Here fortune again favoured them, and they took a prisoner who informed them that he was one of a party of sixty that had been sent from Fort Stanwix to destroy their boats. Falling ill on the march he had been left behind by them that morning.

Johnson instantly directed a detachment to proceed in pursuit, and march night and day until they overtook the enemy. These instructions were so successfully executed that only two of the Americans escaped from being killed and fifty-two captured. Six mounted Rangers were then sent to intercept two Oneidas whom the enemy had despatched to search for the boats. To their great relief they found their boats un-harmed, and on the 25th the whole column came up and embarked, arriving at Oswego next day. Including Indians, Johnson reported that he had lost nine killed, two wounded, and fifty-two missing, of whom several were known to have been wounded.

Eighteen of the missing men were Rangers, but most of these, headed by Capt. George Dame, returned to Oswego a few days after the main body had sailed away. There they found a boat and a sup-ply of provisions which had been left behind for them, and reached Carleton Island in safety. By the arrival of this party the total loss on the expedition was diminished to forty-six, and a number of stragglers were afterwards brought in by the Indians. Their course was marked by a wide tract of perfect desolation where many smiling farms had been. Johnson stated that thirteen grist mills, numerous saw mills, a thousand houses, and as many barns containing 600,000 bushels of grain, had been given to the flames during the terrible three days spent in marching down Schoharie and up the Mohawk. The severity and importance of the blow was freely admitted by Washington in a letter to the President of Congress of the 7th November:

> The destruction of the grain upon the western frontier of New York is likely to be attended with the most alarming conse-quences, in respect to the formation of magazines upon the North River. We had prospects of forming a very considerable magazine of flour in that quarter previous to the late incursion. The settlement of Schoharie alone would have delivered eighty

thousand bushels of grain, but that fine district is now totally destroyed. I should view this calamity with less concern did I see the least prospect of obtaining the necessary supplies of flour from the States of Pennsylvania, Deleware, and Maryland, previous to the interruption of transportation by frost and bad weather.

In the retreat, Lieut. George McGinn of the Indian department had a most remarkable escape. Badly wounded in the knee in the last action, he was conveyed on horseback with extreme difficulty as far as New Oneida. In the confusion caused by the report that the enemy had sent a party to destroy the boats, he was left behind. A party of nine men was then sent back to bring him off. They carried him a few miles into the woods, and being suddenly alarmed abandoned him with a companion named Mannerly. There these unfortunate men remained exposed to the weather without the least shelter for eleven days, living entirely upon a few handfuls of hickory nuts they managed to collect, until they were discovered by a band of Senecas returning from the war. These Indians carried McGinn to their village at the Genessee, where he lay for two months between life and death before he recovered sufficient strength to admit of his removal to Niagara.

A sudden attack upon the Shawanese villages near the Ohio compelled Capt. Peter Hare to march to their relief with the Rangers stationed at Detroit. Their appearance restored the spirits of those Indians who had been at first inclined to abandon their country. A month later. Hare retired to the Miami, where he built a blockhouse and continued to send scouting parties to the Ohio River until all danger of an invasion had passed.

During the summer of this year Gen. Haldimand took active steps for the formation of settlements both at Detroit and Niagara. In a letter dated the 17th of March, 1780, Lord G. Germain had approved of his scheme. He then took advantage of Col. Butler's visit to Quebec in June to discuss the best method of carrying his proposals into effect. The result was announced in a letter to Col. Bolton of the 7th July:

Having maturely reflected upon the vast expense, uncertainty, and difficulties attending the transport of provisions to the Upper Posts, and for the better accommodation and support of His Majesty's loyal subjects, who, driven from their homes, take refuge at Niagara, I am come to a resolution to reclaim the land granted by the Missassaugas to Sir William Johnson for the Crown, situated on the south-west of the river opposite to the fort, directions of which will be communicated to you by another letter, which land will be divided into several lots and distributed to such loyalists who are capable of improving them and desirous of procuring by industry a comfortable maintenance for their families until such times as by peace they shall be restored to their respective homes, should they be inclined to quit their situation at Niagara.

As the above mentioned grant of land will be reclaimed at the expense of the government, and of course remain at all times the sole property of the Crown and annexed to the fort, those who settle upon it are not to consider that they have the smallest right to any part thereof, the produce alone being their property. They will hold their possessions from year to year, which will be granted by the Commander-in-Chief for the time being, according to their merits. If at any time they should remove, either from inclination or by the order of the commanding officer, they are to have permission to dispose of their crops, stock of cattle, &c., and a reasonable allowance will be made them for their improvements.

For their further encouragement no rent will be required of them. They will be allowed a reasonable quantity of provisions for the space of twelve months after they are put in possession of their lots. Seed, mills, ploughs, and other implements of husbandry will be furnished them *gratis*, and you will please to afford them every assistance, whether of horses or otherwise, as shall be in your power, to those whose sobriety, industry, and good conduct may entitle to such indulgencies.

Some part of the land being already cleared and all of it being fertile, it is expected that in a short time the produce will be considerable. The settlers are therefore to understand that the produce of their farms, over and above their own consumption, is not to be removed from the post, but disposed of to the commanding officer for the use of the troops, and not to traders or accidental travellers.

On the 13th July, he wrote again in these terms:

By my letter of the 7th inst., which will be delivered to you by Lieut.-Col. Butler, you will be made acquainted with my intentions of settling families at Niagara for the purpose of reclaiming and cultivating land to be annexed to the fort. The expediency of this measure is sufficiently evident, not only by the injury the service has and must always suffer from a want of a sufficient supply of provisions, as well as for the present unavoidable consumption of the Indians as for the support of the troops it may be necessary occasionally to march into that country, but likewise to diminish the expense and labour attending so difficult and distant a transport.

I am therefore come to a resolution to extend the scheme to the several posts in the upper country, it already being in some forwardness at Carleton Island, and I here enclose instructions for carrying it into execution at Detroit, which you will please forward to the commanding officer after having perused them. And you will give such orders and assistance as you will judge expedient for promoting with the utmost despatch an undertaking so apparently beneficial to government as well as to the ease and comfort of the troops.

Lieut. Col. Butler, with whom I have conversed fully upon this subject, has promised to give you every assistance in his power, and from his knowledge of farming, his being upon the spot with his Rangers, and his acquaintance and influence with those who may be found to settle, I am persuaded you will find him very useful. I have conversed freely with him upon this subject and have desired him to engage any loyalists he may find proper persons about Montreal and to take them up with him. He informs me there are some good farmers in his corps who, either advancing in years or having a large family, he could dispense with.

You will probably find them fit persons to employ, the more so as they are likely to have assistance from their comrades, but amongst that sort of people little can be expected without a gratuity, and as that business must be done by volunteers and fatigue men, I request that you furnish Col. Butler from the King's store a sufficient quantity.

On the 17th December, Butler reported progress:

The winter wheat sent up for planting came too late. I have returned it into the Commissary's store as provision, fearing the mice would destroy it. I have got four or five families settled and they have built themselves houses. They will want about sixty bushels of spring wheat and oats, and twelve of buckwheat, and a barrel of Indian corn, early in the spring for planting.

The harness sent up is not of the kind wanted, but if dressed leather was sent I would get some of the Rangers to make it. The forge Capt. Twiss was to have sent is not arrived. Please put him in mind of it,

Several small parties were sent out in January, 1781, to gain intelligence and to seek recruits for two additional companies that Butler had obtained permission to raise. The settlements upon the Mohawk River above Johnstown had been literally blotted out of existence by their repeated incursions, and nothing remained but the blank walls of the forts that had failed to protect them. They were accordingly obliged to travel much further and to carry with them three or four weeks' provisions. One party led by Butler's nephew, Lieut. Andrew Bradt, penetrated into New Jersey and returned with fifteen recruits. Others went to Norman's Kill and Hellebergh, even sending their spies into the streets of Albany. They were very successful in obtaining recruits in that quarter, although frequently pursued.

On the 1st February, Brant and Lieut. John Bradt, with thirty Rangers and many Indians, marched to blockade Fort Stanwix. They arrived there just a day too late to intercept a convoy of provisions which they had hoped to take, but cut off a foraging party of seventeen men. A few weeks later another detachment of about the same number fell into their hands, and any man that ventured to show himself outside the walls did so at imminent peril of becoming a mark for a hidden rifleman. Successive parties continued to hover about and harass the garrison in this way until the middle of May, when the fort was burned and abandoned in sheer despair.

Fort Pitt had been blockaded during the winter and spring in like manner, and a good many of the garrison killed or taken. In April Lieut. Bowen burned the deserted fort at Cherry Valley, and destroyed a settlement at Bowman's Creek. Encouraged by these events, their incursions were extended still further. Volunteer Allen led a party into Sussex County, New Jersey, where he burned several mills and alarmed a wide stretch of country for weeks, finally retiring with several prisoners and loyalists. In May there were five scouting parties in different parts of the Mohawk Valley, and one of these even appeared in the outskirts of Schenectady.

Solitary Rangers had been lurking in various places since December, with orders to remain in hiding until something of consequence occurred, when they were to return with all haste to Niagara. The fact that they were not only able to pass constantly through the enemy's country in every direction with absolute impunity, but even to reside there for months together, proves at once that they were in the highest degree active, courageous and resourceful, and that they still had numbers of loyal friends and sympathizers among the inhabitants. If they were taken, they well knew that their fate would not be pleasant to think upon.

On the 3rd of June, Lieut. Robt. Nelles, who had been scouting for several weeks along the western frontier of Pennsylvania with forty men, met an equal number of the local militia and Rangers on the high road, within three miles of Frankstown, in Bedford County, where there was a garrison. In the skirmish that followed thirteen Americans were killed, seven taken prisoners, and five others were wounded, and only got off with the assistance of a party sent out from the fort to their relief Nelles had but one man killed and two wounded. This event spread indescribable terror through all the surrounding country. The lieutenant of the county wrote ten days later:

> This county is in a deplorable situation; a number of families are flying away daily since the late damage. I can assure your Excellency that if immediate assistance is not sent to this county the whole of the frontier will move off in a few days.

In New York very vigorous measures had been undertaken by the Governor for the defence of the frontier. After the destruction of Fort Stanwix, Colonel Willett was placed in command of all troops stationed on the Mohawk. He brought with him two Continental regiments, and fixed his headquarters at Canajoharie. He reported that the militia of the district had been reduced from 2,500 to 800. He estimated that one-third of the missing men had been killed or taken in the various raids, one-third had deserted to the enemy, and the remainder had removed into the interior. Between Schenectady and the German Flats, a distance of sixty-three miles, there were no less than twenty-four forts, each sheltering from ten to fifty families. "Yet, if they succeed in preserving the gain they have in the ground," he added, "they will have an immense quantity more than will be sufficient for their own consumption." For their protection he proposed to keep small bodies of soldiers constantly marching to and fro, and frequently changing their route.

He was not long allowed to remain unoccupied. About the first of June Lieut. John Dochstader marched from Niagara with 70 men. On the 7th he encountered a scout of American riflemen near Otsego Lake, of whom one was killed and another taken. On the 9th two more prisoners were captured, and he arrived at Corrystown, eleven miles from Willett's headquarters. Being fired upon from some fortified houses, these were instantly forced and ten of the inmates killed. Twenty houses were burned, and Dochstader began his retreat, taking with him six prisoners and 120 horses and cattle. Columns of smoke from the burning settlement announced its fate to Willett, and in an hour he had 70 militia in pursuit, "so keen were they for revenge." Before night he followed with 170 soldiers.

Early in the morning, he got in front of Dochstader's party and formed an ambuscade. This movement was discovered and Willett found himself suddenly attacked with "much noise and spirit." After the skirmish had continued for some time, Dochstader perceived that his men were greatly outnumbered and gave the signal to retreat, which was accomplished with the loss of only five wounded, but nearly the whole of the captured cattle were abandoned. Willett had lost fifteen killed and wounded, Capt. McKean, a very active partisan, being, among the former, but thought that he had gained a victory worth boasting of.

In July, Caldwell proceeded from Niagara with a large party in the direction of Schenectady, with some intention of uniting with a detachment which was supposed to be advancing towards that place from Crown Point. On the 3rd of August he overtook another detachment headed by Lieut. John Hare, and they determined to advance together. Their combined force numbered 87 Rangers and 250 Indians. Their provisions being nearly exhausted, the Indians held a council, and without consulting Caldwell, determined to attack a place called Monbackers, or Rochester, in Ulster County. Four days later tracks were discovered, which Caldwell conjectured to be those of a recruiting party of the Rangers.

Lieut. Nelles was sent to reconnoitre, but fell in with a scout of the enemy, which he dispersed and made two prisoners. They were then within forty miles of a small fort at Lackawaxen, commanding a narrow gorge among the hills, which they would be forced to pass on their way. This place Caldwell wished to attack, as the garrison was small, but the Indians positively refused on the ground that it would alarm the country, but promised to attempt its capture on their return.

They passed it in the night without being seen, and on the 11th stole past another fort at Neversink in the same manner. They then entered the outskirts of a flourishing and extensive settlement projected by six strong forts. In attacking these, five Indians were killed or wounded, but one of the forts was then abandoned, which they destroyed, with two mills and thirty stone houses, in one of which a party of men perished after having stubbornly refused to surrender. Many cattle and horses were taken and great quantities of grain destroyed. The Indians were sated with plunder and refused to advance further.

Caldwell sent a party of Rangers to Nipenack, where they burned two mills and many houses and advanced to Monbackers, which they entirely destroyed. They were then within twelve miles of Esopus (Kingston), and the whole country was rising in arms around them. Already two regiments of militia were advancing from opposite quarters to intercept their retreat. Caldwell leisurely retired, driving before him a numerous herd of cattle, in the hope of enticing his pursuers into the woods. But repeated disasters had taught them caution and he was allowed to escape without having a single Ranger injured. Again the misconduct of his Indians placed him in serious peril.

> On our return, (he wrote to Butler), We had the mortification to see the Indians kill and take the greatest part of the cattle captured by the Rangers, which would have left us in a starving condition were it not for the horses we had taken.

On the 8th September, Lieut. John Clement and a chief named Traquanda, with 74 Rangers and Indians, arrived at the German Flats and reconnoitred the fort. Next morning three alarm guns were fired by the garrison, and they concluded that their presence had been discovered. A young Indian, who was sent to watch the fort, returned with the information that forty riflemen were rapidly approaching. They at once abandoned their camp and concealed themselves among the thickets nearby, lying flat on the ground in a semi-circle around the spot. The Americans were headed by Captain Woodworth, who was well known to many of the Rangers as a brave and enterprising enemy. They came boldly on, and when they arrived at the place where the fires had been made Clement heard their leader exclaim, "Damn them! They are gone off!" Clement's men allowed them to approach within pistol shot of the centre of their position, when they fired a single fatal volley and rushed upon them with spears and tomahawks. Woodworth, with two other officers and nineteen men, were killed on the spot, and eight others taken prisoners, while only two Indians were wounded.

At this time the company of Rangers that had been sent to Detroit were actively engaged in repelling what had threatened to be a formidable attack. Encouraged by the easy conquest of Kaskaskias and Vincennes, Col. George Rogers Clark had begun to plan the capture of that place also. His project was warmly supported by Washington, who declared that the "reduction of Detroit is the only means of giving peace and security to our western frontier." Clark felt confident of his ability to enlist a sufficient number of volunteers for the purpose, if he was provided by Congress with artillery and stores. To this Washington not only readily consented, but ordered the commandant at Fort Pitt to detach a company of artillery and as many regular infantry as he could spare to accompany him.

Rumours of Clark's intentions soon reached Detroit. In March Captain Matthew Elliott with a small party made an incursion into Kentucky, and burned a magazine of provisions. He reported that the inhabitants were "night and day employed in removing their effects to a large settlement called Bryant's Station[2], (Bryan's Station), where they hope to remain in security during the expedition." Capt. Thompson then proceeded with the Rangers to their former station at Miami, and Brant went to Detroit with a few warriors of the Six Nations, to inspirit the Indians in that quarter. Brodhead advanced from Fort Pitt and destroyed the Deleware villages, and threatened the Wyandots.

This movement first drew the Rangers to Lorimier's at the portage, between the Great and Little Miami, and then to Sandusky, where they remained for nearly two months encamped among fever haunted swamps. Their spies kept them minutely informed of Clark's movements. Finally about the middle of August they learned that his preparations for the expedition at Wheeling appeared to be nearly completed, and began their long march overland to intercept him on his voyage down the Ohio. On the 26th an advanced party of Indians, commanded by Brant and George Girty, reached the river and captured one of his boats.

From the prisoners they learned that Clark, with the main body, had already passed down the stream, but that a second division was behind. This consisted of 100 Rangers and volunteers in thirteen boats, commanded by Col. Lochry, lieutenant of Westmoreland County, Pa.

---

2. *Siege of Bryan's Station and The Battle of Blue Licks* by Reuben T. Durrett, Bennett H. Young, Henry T. Stanton and George W. Ranck also published by Leonaur.

A few hours later this party came in sight, was enticed ashore, and lured into an ambush with the inevitable result. Lochry, six other officers, and thirty men were killed, twelve officers and fifty-two privates were taken prisoners. Not a man escaped. The Rangers, who had been delayed by heavy rains, then came up, and the whole force floated down the river in the captured boats, with the intention of attacking Clark at the Falls, (Louisville, Ky.,) where he had built a fort. But the Indians, satisfied with this partial success, began to disperse rapidly, and when they arrived within thirty miles of Clark's position only two hundred remained.

Scouts returned from the Falls with some prisoners, who reported that Clark had abandoned the expedition against Detroit. The Shawanese, who were acting as guides, then concluded that it would not be prudent to attack the fort, and as the Rangers had already been four days without provisions, Capt. Thompson marched towards their villages in the hope of obtaining a supply. His men were absolutely at the point of starvation when they succeeded in shooting a couple of bears.

McKee and Brant crossed over into Kentucky and advanced towards Boone's fort. They met and routed a party of horsemen with considerable loss. Next day a larger party, commanded by Col. Floyd, lieutenant of the county, came to the scene of the action to bury the dead. They rode straight into an ambush prepared for them, and most of them were killed or taken, with the loss of only four Indians. Floyd and several other principal officers were among the slain. This concluded active operations in that quarter, but the Rangers remained in the Indian country until all danger of invasion seemed over. For several weeks they subsisted entirely on green corn, and when they finally returned to Detroit their clothing was completely torn to rags in their long marches through the woods.

In September the tenth company of Rangers was completed and pronounced by Col. Powell, after inspection, to be a very good one. A few days after a letter was received from Gen. Haldimand, proposing another raid in force on the same lines as that of the year before. In reply Powell said:

> The Mohawk has been so long the theatre of action for troops and Indians, both from this part and Carleton Island, that very few remain for further operations, for the people have been so much accustomed to those operations that they now secure

what grain they raise in fortified houses, where it would be inexpedient to attack them. Col. Johnson and Col. Butler, who are well acquainted with that part of the country, advise that the force sent out should be assembled at Oswego and proceed to the falls and some island on the south side of Oneida Lake, where the boats might be left under a guard, and from thence to the Tienderha River, whence a party might be sent to destroy the remaining mills at Canajoharie, and afterwards join the main body at Cobus Kill. They might then proceed to Duanesboro', a settlement which has not yet been molested.

This plan was approved of by the governor, and orders issued for putting it into execution. The contingent from Niagara consisted of 36 men of the 8th under Lieut. Coote, 169 Rangers under Capt. Walter Butler, and 109 Indians hastily collected and forcibly described as "the dregs of the tribes," commanded by Capt. Tice. Major Ross, who was placed in command of the expedition, brought with him from Carleton Island 207 officers and men, composed of detachments from four different regiments.

The information derived from prisoners and deserters during the early part of the year had been particularly vague and contradictory. Ross had therefore determined to make an attempt to gain more exact and reliable intelligence by means of a spy. For this dangerous service he selected a bright young man named John Servos, formerly "an active rebel," who had been taken prisoner by Sir John Johnson in his last expedition and had since enlisted in his regiment. In May this agent left Carleton Island and surrendered himself to the Americans as a deserter. He was taken by them to Albany and three times closely examined by the governor and a committee, to whom he gave a description of Carleton Island, prepared for the purpose. On his return in August, Ross reported:

I was lucky in my choice. He has been in every fort on the Mohawk River, one excepted, and brought in a detail of the strength of the whole. After fulfilling everything requisite he obtained a pass to go to the Jerseys, but returned to rejoin his regiment a few days ago with six young recruits for Sir John Johnson's 2nd battalion. He says the inhabitants of the Mohawk are in expectation of a visit from Sir John, and in many places are secreting provisions for him.

As on the former occasion, Haldimand moved forward a body of troops to Crown Point, and to make the alarm more general he instructed Col. Powell to send out several small parties of Rangers and Indians from Niagara against various parts of the frontiers of New York and Pennsylvania.

> You will give these parties orders, (he continued), effectively to destroy all kinds of grain and forage, mills. Sec, cattle, and all articles which can contribute to the support of the enemy. They will, as usual, have the strongest injunctions to avoid the destruction of women and children, and every species of cruelty.

A violent gale prevented the detachments from Niagara from reaching Oswego until the 9th October. Major Ross was already there, and began his march next day. On the 17th he left his boats with a guard in a creek falling into Lake Oneida, and marched towards Otsego Lake. Two days later Lieut. Dochstader of the Rangers, who had distinguished himself on so many occasions, died very suddenly. During the march several prisoners were brought in, from whom it was learned that Sir John Johnson had appeared at Crown Point, but that their own movements were as yet undiscovered. On the 23rd they passed through Cherry Valley, and on the evening of the following day reached Corrystown. Owing to the roundabout route they had taken their appearance at that place was as unexpected as if they had sprung out of the earth.

As they hurried forward towards the Mohawk they took a few prisoners, who stated that there were 1,000 men assembled at Schenectady, 500 at Schoharie, and that Col. Willett was at Canajoharie with 400 more. Duanesboro' or Warrensbush, their objective point, lying centrally between these garrisons, was deemed perfectly safe from attack. Ross perceived that he had no time to lose, as in a few hours his presence would be known at all these places. Although his men were already terribly fatigued by eight days' steady marching in very bad weather, and much of the time ankle-deep in mud, he marched all night through incessant rain and over fourteen miles of the worst possible roads. His men struggled gallantly to keep together and not more than a dozen fell behind, worn out by fatigue, and were abandoned to the tender mercies of the enemy.

At three o'clock in the morning of the 25th, they forded the Schoharie, within gunshot of Fort Hunter, and two hours later halted near Warrensbush, where they were allowed to rest on their arms until daybreak. Then the Rangers and Indians were detailed to destroy the settlement, which was seven miles in length, while the remainder of the troops moved along the main road to support them. They found the place totally deserted, for the inhabitants had fled during the night. By ten o'clock they had advanced within twelve miles of Schenectady and every building in sight was in flames, including three mills and a large public magazine. Ross then wheeled about and marched swiftly up the Mohawk, which he forded at Johnstown with much difficulty, as the river was swollen by the rain.

A small party sallied from Fort Johnson to dispute their passage, but the officer in command was killed at the first fire, and his men dispersed. The militia began to gather behind him, and Ross determined to retreat directly through the woods to Carleton Island instead of attempting to return to his boats, but concealed his intention from everybody in order to prevent the enemy from learning it from prisoners or deserters. Marching through the village, he halted in the fields near Johnson Hall. Provisions were hastily collected and cattle slaughtered for the journey without the least molestation.

Willett had advanced from Canajoharie with his whole force at the first alarm, and by marching all night had arrived at Fort Hunter early in the morning. He picked up several stragglers from the regular troops under Ross's command and obtained their estimate of the numbers of the raiders. Already the Schoharie had risen so rapidly that the ford had become impassable and he was obliged to cross in boats. This delayed him until afternoon, and he then learned that Ross had crossed the Mohawk, and followed as rapidly as the roads would permit. He was joined by 400 men from Schenectady, and by detachments from other quarters, which increased his force to more than 1200, much of it, however, being militia and new levies.

At three o'clock in the afternoon, the scouts sent out by Ross returned without having observed any signs of a pursuit, and he directed Captain Tice to lead the way with the Indians by the most direct route to Carleton Island. When Tice had advanced a mile into the woods he was suddenly ordered to return and join the Rangers, who were covering the rear. The enemy was then advancing so rapidly and in such force that Ross was convinced that it would no longer be possible for his jaded troops to outmarch him without sacrificing many of the weaker men, and he determined to fight. He hastily selected a position about a quarter of a mile after entering the woods, and formed a line covered by the Rangers some distance in front. Exclusive of the Indians, who were of little service, he had then 354 of all ranks under arms.

The enemy soon appeared and the Rangers began the action with a volley, which they followed up by charging with their well-known Indian yell, and drove the American riflemen entirely out of the woods. Willett himself came to their support with a large body of infantry, having previously detached nearly a third of his force to turn his opponent's position and cut off his retreat. When Willett's party had fairly entered the woods, Ross ordered a general advance, followed by a charge, which was attended with immediate and entire success. Willett confessed that the whole of his right wing "turned and fled without any apparent cause." Some of his men, however, kept up a running fight until they were driven to the edge of the woods, when the whole body "fled precipitately in full view for more than a mile."

"I then lamented the want of a good body of Indians," Ross complained, "few of those present venturing to engage, or we would probably have crushed the spirit of the rebels on the Mohawk." The left wing of the Americans still remained unbroken, covered by the fire of a field-piece planted upon a high ridge in front, but being briskly charged also gave way, leaving the gun and its ammunition behind.

The victorious troops pursued as rapidly as fatigue would permit, killing many and taking a few prisoners. Before the firing had ended, the third division of the enemy appeared on the edge of the woods in their rear, but "seemed inclined rather to harass than attack openly." They remained under cover, keeping up a desultory fire from their concealment. The field-piece was turned on them, and after a few rounds they were charged and dispersed in their turn. In the pursuit, which was continued for two miles, they suffered severely, and had not darkness intervened would have been nearly exterminated. In this series of skirmishes Ross had not lost more than twenty men in killed and wounded, but the darkness and exhaustion caused many others to stray away and increased his total loss to fifty. He believed that the loss inflicted upon the enemy was very much greater, as he counted twenty of their dead in one place and he had secured twenty-four prisoners.

Willett collected his scattered forces and retired across the bridge at Johnstown, where he took possession of the stone church. Ross marched six miles into the woods and encamped for the night. Next day he continued his retreat unpursued, but successive storms of snow and sleet prevented him from gaining the trail leading from the German Flats to Carleton Island until the evening of the 29th, and it was then discovered that the Indians had shaped their course to favour their own return to Niagara, instead of considering the safety of the troops, Disgusted by this final proof of their misconduct, he resolved to allow them to go their own way, and marched early on the following morning, leaving them still shivering over their smouldering fires. But, when all danger appeared to be over, the pursuer was actually close at his heels.

Willett had hurried directly from the late battlefield to the German Flats, and sent men to find and destroy his opponent's boats. He collected 500 fresh troops, including 60 Oneida Indians, and appears to have divined that Ross was retreating directly to Carleton Island. On the 29th he crossed the river with this force very lightly equipped, and followed the trail in search of traces of his march. At night he had actually encamped within a couple of miles of the exhausted fugitives. Soon after daylight he surprised some of the Indians who still lingered in camp, and took Lieut. Ryckman. The first intimation of this event was conveyed to Ross by riflemen firing on his rear.

At this he ordered his men to move on as rapidly as possible until they had crossed Canada Creek, when they would make a final stand. A few of the Rangers halted to engage the pursuers and the remainder went on at a trot in Indian file. After crossing the creek Capt. Butler, who had gallantly commanded the covering party, lined the ford with Rangers to gain time for his leader to choose a position. The stream and all surrounding objects were veiled in dense fog, when Willett's advance guard came up and plunged without hesitation into the water. For a moment, the fog parted and they saw Butler wave his hand in defiance, and a volley from the opposite bank struck down several of their number. The survivors scrambled hastily up the bank and retreated into the woods.

The fog settled down again and several volleys were interchanged at random across the creek. One of these chance shots struck Capt. Butler in the head and he instantly fell dead where he stood. Perceiving that the Americans had a decided advantage in the ground "and their favourite object of firing at a distance," Ross had taken up a better position a quarter of a mile further on, where he awaited an attack for an hour before continuing his retreat. When the firing ceased Willett crossed the stream and found Butler and three Rangers lying dead but did not venture to pursue further. The wonderful endurance displayed by his opponents excited his frank admiration. "Although they had been four days in the wilderness," he said, "with only half a pound of horseflesh a day per man, yet they ran in their famished condition thirty miles before they stopped." He exulted loudly over Butler's death, and his biographer tells us that the inhabitants generally rejoiced more on learning that than they did at the intelligence of the surrender of Cornwallis, which became known to them about the same time.

In the pursuit and skirmish Ross had actually lost only ten men and although he had yet seven days march before him through a barren wilderness, intersected by several streams passable only by means of rafts, although the weather was most inclement, and his men were almost without food and many of them had lost their blankets and overcoats, he arrived at Carleton Island on the 6th November without further loss, and even carrying with him the whole of his prisoners. In the whole expedition he had lost 74 officers and men, two-thirds of whom were returned as missing. Thirteen of these were Rangers, who subsequently returned in safety to Oswego. Some of the missing men who were so unfortunate as to have fallen into the hands of their exasperated enemies appear to have been put to death in cold blood, with an excess of cruelty. Benton, in his *History of Herkimer County*, states that one non-commissioned officer was given up to the Oneidas, and in one of Haldimand's letters there is a horrible story of a Ranger being gradually dismembered by his captors while he was yet alive.

The Rangers returned to Niagara for the winter. In their absence Caldwell had gone to Detroit to relieve Capt. Thompson, and the latter had been accidentally drowned when on his way down.

The progress of the Niagara settlement during the year was briefly sketched in Butler's correspondence.

On the 20th of May he said:—

The articles you mentioned for the loyalists I have received and given out to such as had lands ready to sow. The farmers are much in need of a blacksmith and forge and iron, such as is fit for plough-shares, as there are still a few wanted for farmers already settled. Iron fit for axes, hoes, &c., is also wanting. I can furnish them with a smith out of the Rangers, who will be obliged to work for what the king allows. I should imagine if His Excellency thinks proper to allow the above articles for one year, they might after that be able to help themselves. I believe but one family draws provision, the rest have been able to help themselves.

On the 7th December, he resumed the subject:

> The winter being so moderate here enables the farmers to clean
> the ground and prepare it for planting and sowing early in the
> spring. If they only begin to cultivate the land in summer, the
> season is over before they can expect to draw any subsistence
> from their labour. I flatter myself that in a short time the farm-
> ers will be found to be of essential use to this post. They have
> maintained themselves since September last, and were only al-
> lowed half-rations from the first.

Elsewhere the war was practically at an end. Both troops and Indians were much dispirited by the surrender of Lord Cornwallis. Still,
several small parties of Rangers remained on the frontier the whole
winter, and continued to be joined by fresh recruits in spite of the
gloomy prospect.

In April nearly 200 Rangers were detached to Carleton Island to
enable Major Ross to occupy Oswego, and a party of picked men
from these, under Sergeant Secord, went with him to act as scouts.

On the 15th of the same month, Lieut. R. Nelles, scouting on the
frontier of Pennsylvania, took and destroyed a blockhouse on Bald Ea-
gle Creek. Orders were then received to abstain as far as possible from
offensive operations, and no expedition was undertaken until June,
when Capt. Powell and Sangerachta marched towards Fort Pitt to create a diversion in favour of the Western Indians, who were then menaced with a formidable attack from that quarter. This party destroyed
the fort and settlement of Loyal Hanna, on the road to Philadelphia,
and took about thirty prisoners.

The want of active employment and the conviction now forced
upon them that their cause was lost, told severely upon the spirits of
the provincial troops generally during this period. Major Ross has
forcibly described the temptations and misgivings that beset them.

> The colony troops, (he said), have not that relish for the war
> they had when carried on offensively. They do not think the
> King will succeed. From every quarter they have unpleasing
> tidings. Their little properties on the Mohawk River are taken
> possession of by the New Englanders. They conclude the best
> chance they have now is to make peace with the rebels. Desert-
> ers they know are received and live quiet at home. I'll venture
> to say that there are many men who would sooner have suf-
> fered death than desert some time ago, that nothing now but

fear of death prevents. In short, their spirits are low.

The Rangers, however, were much less affected by this depression than other regiments that had not been so actively engaged, possibly because they had for years entertained small hopes of any reconciliation.

In the west a body of Rangers was actively employed during the summer, with signal success. Early in the year a party of frontiersmen had made a descent upon a village on the Muskingum, solely inhabited by Indians converted to Christianity by the Moravian missionaries. They had taken no part in the war, it was admitted, but were accused of having harboured hostile Indians. It was determined to kill all the prisoners on the spot. Two of the largest buildings were selected as "slaughter-houses;" the helpless victims were dragged in with ropes around their necks, and ninety-six persons, of whom two-thirds were women and children, were brutally beaten to death. The bodies were then burnt in the houses.

Elated by the ease with which they had accomplished this foul deed, they declared their intention of marching against Sandusky and repeating their exploit there. By the middle of May their design was known in Detroit, and Caldwell with his company and the "Lake Indians" was ordered to march to the assistance of the Indians at that place, who were much alarmed. Lieut. Turney, with twenty-four Rangers from Niagara, joined him soon after his arrival at Sandusky. They soon learned that 500 mounted riflemen, including most of those concerned in the late massacre, were already marching against them. Swift-footed runners hovered about them as they advanced.

They counted their numbers, and learned from writing on the trees and on scraps of paper scattered about their deserted camps that they intended to give no quarter to man, woman, or child. Even their friends admitted that they were generally animated by no other motive than a desire for murder and plunder, although their leader. Col. Crawford, was a brave and honourable man. Several Continental officers from the garrison of Fort Pitt accompanied the expedition as a "party of pleasure." The entire force was well armed and finely mounted, and was not without experience in Indian warfare. They were in high spirits and sanguine of success.

To meet them Caldwell had 70 Rangers, 44 Lake Indians, and the whole fighting strength of the Wyandots of Sandusky, numbering not more than 150 warriors, young and old. McKee, who had gone to bring up the Shawanese to their assistance, was daily expected to return.

At noon on the king's birthday, the 4th of June, 1782, Caldwell learned that the enemy were only a few miles away, and he at once advanced to meet them at the junction of the two paths, where he could protect either of the Indian villages from attack at the same time. On his appearance, Crawford retired into a large grove of copse-wood, surrounded on all sides by open ground, which furnished good cover for horses and men, and gave him a decided advantage until the Rangers managed to gain a foothold in a projecting angle of woods, and gradually pushed back their antagonists until Caldwell was able to place most of his force under cover. The skirmish then became very brisk, with a prodigious amount of yelling and firing on both sides, but little loss on either. Caldwell, however, was soon badly wounded by a musket ball, which passed through both his thighs, and forced him to quit the field.

The command then devolved on Lieut. John Turney, a veteran soldier of many years service, while Capt. Matthew Elliott directed the movements of the Indians. They continued to gain ground until night put an end to the firing. The Americans had lost about twenty-five men, their assailants only five or six. Both parties encamped where they lay, and at daybreak Turney renewed the attack, but observed that the enemy seemed reluctant to continue the action. However, they made two feeble attempts to charge, which were easily repulsed. At noon McKee opportunely arrived with 140 Shawanese, and enabled Turney to surround the Americans.

Throughout the afternoon he continued to press his advantage, and at dark felt sanguine of capturing the whole body. Probably he would have succeeded if the Indians had not directed their sentries to fire at stated intervals during the night. This indicated the weakest part of the line to the enemy, and at midnight they made a vigorous rush upon it and broke through. Most of them were mounted and darkness favoured their flight, but they were pursued with the tireless energy born of insatiable hate. The chase continued many days, and the last man that fell beneath the tomahawk of the Indians was struck down on the very banks of the Ohio.

Caldwell and McKee estimated that 250 of the fugitives were killed or perished in the woods. The unfortunate Crawford and a few others were reserved for a worse fate. They were horribly tortured to death in spite of the remonstrances of the only Indian officer present. Caldwell said that Crawford "died like a hero, and never changed countenance," although suffering the most dreadful agony. In consequence of this atrocious act of revenge, Maj. De Peyster threatened to withdraw the Rangers from the support of the Indians in case the offence was repeated.

> I must, therefore, reiterate my injunctions to you, (he wrote to McKee), of representing to the chiefs that such a mode of war will by no means be countenanced by their English father, who is ever ready to assist them against the common enemy, provided they avoid cruelties. Tell them I shall be under the necessity of recalling the troops, (who must be tired of such scenes of cruelty,) provided they persist.

In the two days' skirmishing but one Ranger was killed and two wounded, besides Capt. Caldwell. Of the Indians, interpreter Le Vallier and four warriors were killed and eight warriors wounded.

> Too much cannot be said in praise of the officers and men and Indians, (Turney wrote). No people could behave better. Capt. Elliott and Lieut. Clench in particular signalized themselves.

From the prisoners it was learned that Col. Clark still meditated an attack upon the Shawanese villages, in which he had been so signally baffled the year before. Those Indians at once became urgent in their demands that the Rangers should move to their assistance. Caldwell recovered rapidly from his wounds and resumed command. On the 12th July he marched from Upper Sandusky with the intention of assailing Wheeling, and had actually advanced as far as the Whetstone branch of the Scioto, when he was diverted to the Shawanese village of Piqua by the report that it was menaced with an attack. McKee had succeeded in assembling upwards of 1,100 Indians for its defence, but on finding that there was no occasion for alarm they began to disperse rapidly. Caldwell and McKee, with the Rangers and 300 Indians, advanced to the Ohio, and on the 15th of August crossed that river and marched upon Bryant's Station, the principal fort in Kentucky. They besieged it unsuccessfully for two days, but destroyed everything outside the walls.

On retreating along the "Great Buffalo Trail" about a hundred Indians broke off by another route, and left Caldwell with thirty Rangers and only 200 Wyandot and Lake Indians. He then turned aside to the Blue Licks, where the ground would be more favourable for an action, and encamped in a grassy hollow near the ford of the Licking River. Early in the morning of the 18th his scouts announced that about 200 of the enemy were rapidly approaching on horseback. These were picked men from the Kentucky settlements, all splendidly mounted, commanded by Cols. Todd, Trigg, Daniel Boone, and other well known leaders. They dismounted and crossed the ford on foot. When within sixty yards a single shot was fired from the Rangers' covert in the long grass, to which they instantly replied with an entire volley. Caldwell said, "They stood to it very well for some time, till we rushed in upon them, when they broke immediately." All resistance was at an end in five minutes.

"He that could mount a horse was well off; he that could not had no time for delay," wrote one of the few survivors. Caldwell stated that 146 were killed or taken including nearly all the principal officers. Not a Ranger was hurt and only six Indians were killed and ten wounded. The interpreter La Bute, was also killed. "He died like a warrior," Caldwell said, "fighting arm to arm. The Indians behaved extremely well, and no people could behave better than both officers and men in general."

Capt. Andrew Bradt having arrived at Sandusky with his company of Rangers too late to overtake Caldwell, had marched against Wheeling, accompanied by 238 Indians. On the 11th September he devastated the settlement there, and ten days later joined Caldwell in the Shawanese country, where they remained for about a month Hunger, exposure, and disease did their work, and when they returned to Detroit the commandant spoke of them as "walking spectres."

The infant colony at Niagara continued to make a rather feeble growth.

On the 4th April, Col. Powell reported that "the farmers are clearing some ground on the other side of the river to plant corn for government, and as there is some exceeding good land cleared at Buffalo Creek, Col. Butler has advised me to plant some there and a party shall accordingly be sent, but I am afraid no great progress can be made in farming this year." At midsummer he stated that the farmers had scarcely raised grain enough for their own consumption. Butler took a more cheerful view On the 12th June he wrote :

I am happy His Excellency is pleased with the progress of the farmers. They certainly have done very well, and would have done much better had they received smithy tools, provisions,

&c., the want of which has disappointed them, as they expected to be supplied agreeable to the memorandum His Excellency gave me.

Seven or eight Rangers got their families from the frontier last fall. These, with some others that have been here for some time are desirous of being discharged and leave to settle on lands near the place, provided they can be supplied with provisions for one year and such smith work as may be necessary. These people were bred farmers, and I am of opinion will soon be useful to this post, as well as to enable them to support their families comfortably, which at present is very difficult.

I daily expect a number of recruits from the frontier, which will enable me to keep my corps complete after discharging those people that are in the decline of life and having large families.

In the same letter, he stated that Peter and James Secord were preparing to build a saw and grist mill near the Rangers' Barracks. They intended to buy the iron work and millstones in Lower Canada, and wished to have these sent up in the King's ships. He was informed, in reply, that the private ownership of the mill would not be permitted, but that materials would be furnished and the Secords paid for working it.

An official survey of the 25th August showed that there were sixteen families settled, numbering sixty-eight persons. They had cleared 236 acres, and had raised during the year 206 bushels of wheat, 46 of oats, 926 of Indian corn, and 630 of potatoes. They owned 49 horses, 42 cows, 30 sheep, and 103 hogs.

In November, Col. Allan Maclean, who had succeeded to the command of the garrison, wrote that:

Lieut. Brass, formerly Sergeant Brass, now employed to build a corn and saw mill, says he will undertake to complete the dam and finish the two mills at the expense of £500, N.Y. currency, or to be paid so much a day for the time employed, as he is to be chief workman himself.

Col. Butler had been seriously ill for several weeks, and Maclean seized the opportunity to pay a warm tribute to his ability.

Butler, (he said), recovers but slowly. He is the only man here equal in any degree to the management of the Indians. It is surprising in what good humour he sent them away after he had acquainted them that he was short of several articles of clothing for them this year.

Butler was sufficiently recovered in the spring to resume his labours. On the 3rd of March he wrote:—

The farmers actually settled here are not well satisfied with the uncertain tenure on which they hold their lands and improvements, and would rather be subject to a small rent if they could be more effectually secured to them. Should this be done I am satisfied there are some people of that description who have even property in the colonies that would not think of returning.

The saw and grist mills are both in forwardness, and if the materials from below arrive in time I imagine may be set going by the beginning of June.

The discontent of the settlers soon found a voice in the following petition:

To John Butler, Esq., Lt. Col. commandant of the corps of Rangers, &c.:—

The humble address of farmers residing on lands on the west side the River Niagara;

On our first settling, you were pleased to read to us His Excellency General Haldimand's proposals, on which we settled, and expecting one year's provisions and a blacksmith to work for us, which we have not had as yet. Part only of the provisions has been given us. We shall regard it as a singular favour to lay this before Brig. Gen. Maclean. We should be forever obliged to His Excellency if he will be pleased to grant us leases, or some other security for our farms, as our present uncertain situation is very discouraging, as we are obliged to sell our produce, what little we raise, at such price as the commanding officer thinks proper.

We have no objection to furnish the garrison at a reasonable price what quantity they may want fixed by the commanding officer, at the same time beg leave to sell to merchants and others at the price we can agree, from being obliged to pay merchants their own prices for everything we want. We should be very willing to subject ourselves to a rent for our farms after a term of eight years, as the footing we are on at present we are liable to be turned off our places when the commanding officer pleases. We are happy for the present, being not under the slightest apprehension, but the commandant often changes, which makes our stay uncertain.

Isaac Dolsen,
Elijah Phelps,
Thos McMicking,
Donal Bee,
On behalf of ourselves and the rest of the farmers.

The prospective return of peace inspired the exiles with little hope of being restored to their former homes. In May, 1783, Maclean wrote:—

Col. Butler says that none of his people will ever think of going to attend courts of law in the colonies, where they could not expect the shadow of justice, and that to repurchase their estates is what they are not able to do; that for a much smaller sum the Missassaugas will part with twelve miles more along the lake, and that they would rather go to Japan than go among the Americans, where they could never live in peace.

As soon as the stipulations in their favour, contained in the provisional articles of peace, became generally known, the American newspapers were filled with declarations of undying animosity to the expatriated loyalists, and there could be no doubt that that part of the treaty at least would be openly set at defiance. Of those who had already rashly ventured to return to their former homes, some were executed without form of law, and many savagely assaulted. The remainder were peremptorily warned to leave the country before the 10th of June, under penalty of being treated "with the severity due to their crimes and nefarious defection."

During the summer the entire battalion of Rangers was officially inspected by Major Potts of the 8th regiment, and its appearance and conduct elicited his hearty commendation. •

During the course of the war, upon the service they have been employed they have ever in general behaved bravely and done their duty, and are deserving of whatever His Majesty may be generously pleased to favour or reward them with. . . .

But I must not omit to observe to Your Excellency, that two-thirds of the men are as fine fellows as I ever saw collected together, worthy of applause, and by no means wanting in the requisites to effect in every respect good soldiers, and might, should they be wanted, form a most complete small corps, at 50 men per company, and might answer every purpose that could be wished for to effect the service of the upper country regarding the connection with the Indians.

The late views of great part of the corps was to return to their former homes as soon as a reduction should take place, but from the late publications of the colonists, and the disposition they seem to have avowed to abide by, has much abated the ardour and anxiety of the men on the purpose to return home, and the promises of Col. Butler to obtain some general settlement upon the neighbouring, lands of this lake and river seems to have taken up and engaged both their consideration, hope, wishes, and expectation, that they may succeed in grants of land to that end, which I believe most of them at present are disposed to settle upon.

A return of the corps, showed a strength of 469 men, 111 women, and 257 children. Many of the officers and non-commissioned officers had begun to provide for the future by selecting lands, and the number of acres cleared had already increased to 713.

The regiment was finally disbanded in June, 1784, with the intention that the men should at once take up their residence on lands assigned to them in the immediate vicinity, but there was unforeseen delay in making the surveys and their dissatisfaction with the tenure had not abated.

On the 28th June, Col. De Peyster reported:

The people sign to their desire for cultivating Crown Lands but slowly. We have not above 100 on the list. They seem to dislike the tenure of the lands, and many wish to fetch their relations from the States by the shortest route. I have permitted some of the most decent people to wait Your Excellency's pleasure on that head, but last night seventy of the people who refused to sign went off without leave, with the intent never to return.

However, the great majority decided to remain, and within a month 258 officers and men had agreed to settle, making, with their families, a body of 620 persons.

For a quarter of a century afterwards, the names of officers and men of the disbanded regiment constantly recur in the peaceful annals of their new home as legislators and magistrates, as surveyors and town officers.

Butler's personal influence increased with the flight of time. He was universally regarded as the mainstay of the settlement, and an acknowledged authority on all matters concerning it. Until the formation of the province of Upper Canada, he served as judge of the District Court, and continued to perform the responsible and difficult duties of deputy superintendent of the Indians until his death, in 1796. Successive commandants at Niagara added their testimony as to his tact, zeal, and ability, to that of their predecessors. He retained the confidence and respect of Carleton and Simcoe to the last, and, apart from the spiteful attacks of Claus and Johnson, there is scarcely a hostile criticism of his public or private conduct to be discovered in all the huge mass of official correspondence.

Many of his followers lived to bear arms in the war of 1812, although generally far advanced in years. Barent Frey and John Rowe died gallantly in the held; Thomas Butler fell a victim to disease; William Caldwell, David Secord, Ralfe Clench and John Hardy won honourable distinction for meritorious service. Even in those whose age and infirmities absolutely disabled them from active service the old spirit yet burned so fiercely that they eagerly volunteered to do garrison duty and release younger men to confront the invader.

The Story of Cherry Valley

Henry U. Swinnerton

Contents

The Story of Cherry Valley

Two years ago there was placed in the Presbyterian Church at Cherry Valley a mural tablet, whose inscription recalls the story which I am to relate to you in the briefest form. It reads:

A. D. 1741
Rev. Samuel Dunlop A. B.
a native of Ulster, Ireland,
led hither the families who founded
THIS CHURCH
He here preached God's peace
and taught Liberal Learning
Thirty-seven years
His Work ended in scenes of Blood
His Home desolated, He died in Exile,
near Albany.
cir. 1780.

———

His Wife
Elizabeth (Gallt) Dunlop,
born in Coleraine,
their daughter Mary Wells, her Husband,
and children, save one,
were cruelly slain in the
MASSACRE
which scattered the flock
Nov. 11, 1778.

A short distance from the present church is the ancient cemetery, a scant quarter acre, crowded full of Revolutionary memorials. In it stood the church of that day, a handsome structure then newly built, and about it extended the palisade fort, bastioned for cannon at opposite angles. Within the small area lie the graves of four Revolutionary colonels and upwards of a dozen others, officers and privates and civilian officials, who fought or served in that war; besides quite a multitude of those who suffered death or captivity, or narrowly escaped it with loss of everything at that terrible time.

Around, rough slabs of rock mark the graves of the pioneers who died in the early day when there was no chisel to cut their epitaphs; among them that of John Wells, cultured gentleman and officer in the French War, and lay judge on the bench at Johnstown. Within view of the cemetery all around, are homesteads, each the centre of some tale or tradition of the savage event, and by it passes the earliest thoroughfare trodden by men's feet on this frontier. The place lies on the northernmost terrace of the Catskill highland, twelve miles south of the Mohawk River, 1,400 feet above tide.

From immemorial time a wilderness route had been known to the Indians from the Mohawk at Canajoharie to the head of the Susquehanna, down which stream they passed on war or hunt, to Pennsylvania and the Chesapeake and beyond. From this primitive highway trails led northward up the Unadilla and the Chenango to the heart of the country of the Oneidas and Onondagas; and further west by the Chemung to the hunting grounds and lakes, the villages and "castles" of the Cayugas and Senecas, or Senekees. Early discovering this track, Dutch fur traders found their way to the gathering place for barter, Oghwaga, at the carry across the Great Bend, the largest village on this path. This spot, near Windsor, is important to be noted, as a centre of primitive trade, of early travel, of missionary effort and of war. The name survives in the hamlet of Onoquago, and Tuscarora, across the stream is the site of the village assigned by the Iroquois to a band of that adopted tribe.

No white inhabitant had an abode in all this solitude. Eastward and northward a few German exiles from the Palatinate of the Rhine had begun to settle thinly in the Schoharie Valley, and a little beyond Canajoharie on the Mohawk. In a beautiful depression on this old trail, beyond the rugged ascent to the watershed, and at the spot where the red men launched their canoes in the farthest streams of the Susquehanna, a patent of 8,000 acres was, in 1738, secured by three leading men of Albany, Lendert Gansevoort, Jacob Roseboom and Sybrant Van Schaick, and assigned the following year to their associate, John Lindsay, a Scotchman of enterprise, who brought his family and built a habitation in 1739. After events gave the site, a beautiful knoll, a double interest, when it became the bloodiest scene of the massacre. They were narrowly saved from perishing with hunger in the bitter winter ensuing by the succour of an Indian on snowshoes with food from the river.

In New York Lindsay had enlisted the efforts of a young clergyman, travelling through the colonies, Rev. Samuel Dunlop, through whom were secured a few Presbyterian families from Londonderry, Ireland, who seeking freedom and prospects of greater promise, about 1720, had emigrated to Boston and had founded a new Londonderry in New Hampshire. Finding conditions still unfriendly even in New England, James Campbell, David Ramsay, John Dickson and John Gallt, with their families, in 1741, came to the spot, making the voyage around Cape Cod to New York and up the Hudson by sloop; slowly tacking for two weeks, it is said, on the river.

The sloops sailed under Captain Pruyn, a cousin of the owner, who anxiously awaited its arrival at the wharf, in whose family tradition has preserved the story. The provision of food had been spent, and the voyagers needed immediate aid, which was cordially afforded them. The merchants of Albany appreciated the value of the establishment of a settlement far out on the Susquehanna trail. The ancient ledgers of Hendryck Myndent Roseboom, fur dealer and importer of European merchandise, and his sons, still preserved, show the profitable trade of long years with the people of Cherry Valley, which marked his enlightened liberality in lending them aid when he learned of their exhausted condition, and in furnishing them supplies and tools for their arduous venture.

Hendryck established his son John at Schenectady to be nearer the Indians, while another son, Myndert, remained at Albany, the character of the traffic even down to the advent of the war appears from the entries in their books. For example: "Myndert Roseboom in Albany" debited, Nov. 1774, with an invoice amounting to £210.17.2., enumerating "1361 lbs. of read leather at 2s. 9d per lb., 33 of parchment, 16 otters, 1 fisher, 14 mush rats, 13 gray skins, 9 bareskins, 5 beavers, etc." The surprising extent of the trade in articles of silver will appear from a few of the entries; for John called himself a "silversmith." Messrs Abm. Van Eppes & Jacob Van Epes; 5 arm bands, 3 round moons, 4 pare rist bands, 1 box, 50 pare eare rings, 13 pare large, 100 broaches, 50 do. small — 21.18.0. In Apr. 1773 Gorset Teller & Will'm Groesbeck purchase sueh jewelrey—"eare wheels, large crosses, half-moons, hare plaits, (perhaps like what the Dutch peasant girls wear)—"and 1000 gun flints," to the amount of £115.9.0. [1]

The place had been called Lindsay's Bush, but Mr. Dunlap, writing to his friends, proposed to date his letter from Cherry Valley, from the wild cherry growth everywhere about. On leaving Ireland he had promised Elizabeth Gallt that he would claim her within seven years or leave her free. Having been absent nearly that time, he now returned. Storms delayed the ship off the wild coast, and he arrived just as the date was expiring, and only in time to snatch his bride from a marriage to another. It was a faithful union of long years, to be broken by a tragical end.

Some additional settlers returned with them, but for years the place remained feeble, until the Revolution, the last point of departure and supply for those setting out or returning from the wilderness. The agents of Sir William Johnson 's important traffic with the natives passed to and from Oghwaga through the place; bodies of Palatine Germans took the Susquehanna route to settle its lower valley and become the fathers of the Pennsylvania Dutch;

I and, later, claimants from Connecticut followed, to settle Wyoming and withstand Indian massacre and the Pennamite wars with the partisans of William Penn. Lindsay soon left Cherry Valley and his farm was taken by John Wells, who became a man of influence, and in process of time his son Robert wedded Mr. Dunlop's daughter Mary. Their neighbour was James Willson, who had surveyed the patent and

1. Mr. Roseboom held the responsible position of *Cruyt Magassijn Meester*, or "Powder Master," at Albany continuously from 1771 to 1786, embracing the entire period of the war. His *Powder Book* records "June 10, 1777, 100 barrels, loaded by order of Mr. Philip van Renselaer, 25 wagons each, 4 bar'l" This ammunition was used in the campaign against Burgoyne. The *Receipt Book* of his son. Col. Myndert Roseboom, as one of the "Commissioners, Middle District, Albany," is full of receipts of moneys for food and supplies gathered for "the poor, distressed people" and the "Refugees;" extending from Sept. 16, 1777 to April 2, 1778, the time when the pinch of war was sternly felt in the upper Hudson and Mohawk Valleys.

who had been high sheriff of Albany County. His son seems to have married a second of the daughters, named Eleanor. As early as 1748 missionaries under the influence of Jonathan Edwards at Northampton and Rev. Eleazer Wheelock, who founded a school for Indian youth at Lebanon, Conn., the school in which the able Indian leader, Joseph Brant, received a civilized education, established themselves at Oghwaga and other spots, leading to intercourse with a class of men passing to and fro superior to the usual wayfarer of the wilds, such as John Sergeant and David Brainerd, Elihu Spencer, Samuel Kirkland and the able Gideon Hawley.

Among the unmarked graves in the old cemetery must be that of a young Delaware Indian, pious, educated with Joseph Brant at Lebanon, Joseph Wooley, a preacher, teacher and apostle to his people, who died at Cherry Valley on one of his journeys to the Susquehanna. Mr. Dunlop, being a university man, gathered a few pupils very early whom he taught the classics, following the plough, or in the rude log church and school house reared near the Wells residence. It was the first beginnings of liberal education, as his church was the earliest seat of worship in English west of Albany and the Hudson. Major John Frey, and others prominent in the Revolution, were here educated. All the region southwest of Canajoharie was vaguely known as Cherry Valley, its lake, Otsego, was the Cherry Valley Lake, and the narrow Indian path was gradually subdued and widened into a rugged wagon road, the Cherry Valley road. It followed Bowman's Creek and up the steep of Teckaharawa. Long the little community remained remote and lonely, an outpost of civilization on the southwest verge of the Mohawk's country, with whom and the Oneidas; next west, the most cordial relations were maintained, and for Mr. Dunlop especially the Indians conceived high regard and veneration.

After the first twenty years the immigrants became more numerous, leading to a new issue; scattered settlements began thinly to push out west, southwest and south. At Springfield and on Otsego Lake, on the Butternut Creek and the Unadilla and Charlotte Rivers, and all along the upper Susquehanna, little clearings began to forewarn the Indians that the irresistible white man was slowly occupying his forests. Every settler was a hunter, scouring the woods for game, slaughtering the pigeon roosts and sweeping the streams of their fish. The

Germans were pushing up the Mohawk; by 1750 and '60 beyond the Falls Hill (Little Falls), a strong community had been gathered about the German Flatts, and a string of forts traced a road of growing travel right through the territory of the Oneidas to the lakes. The land of the Mohawks, eastward, had been reduced to scattered patches interspersed among the holdings and great patents of the whites.

The savage freely sold or gave his land, but awoke later to see that his home and his haunts were gone, and his means of subsistence were too slender to be shared with all these newcomers. The intelligent young chief of the tribe, Tha-yen-da-na-gue, by his English name Joseph Brant, enjoyed the entire confidence of Sir William Johnson, co-operating in his enlightened plans and policy in the management of Indian affairs and by procuring them civilized advantages endeavouring to make up to his people what they lost by these changes. In visiting England in the interests of the claims made by the Indians, where the most flattering attentions were shown him by the court and the great officials of the government in London, it came about inevitably that he contracted ties and gained a point of view which naturally made him their ally in any changes which were later to arise.

To stay the discontent of the Indians and fix a limit beyond which the inroads of the settlers should cease, was the object of the Treaty of Fort Stanwix in 1768. Three thousand Indians gathered with their chiefs to meet Sir William Johnson, the king's Indian superintendent, and it was covenanted that the white man should not go west of the Unadilla. That river and a line extended south to the Delaware (co-inciding with the present western boundary of Delaware and Otsego Counties) should be the limit of all further advance of the despoiling settlers. This Indian line was a continental affair; of imperial extent it shut out civilization from the whole Great Lake region, including the western part of New York and the adjoining part of Pennsylvania and the entire north-west territory to the Ohio River. It passed down the Susquehanna and by the Towanda Creek to the Alleghany.

The last parcel of ground on the Susquehanna was taken up at the mouth of the Unadilla in 1770 by a friend of Mr. Dunlop's. Rev. William Johnston, with a colony of his Scotch-Irish compatriots from Duanesburg, driven first from Worcester, Mass., by Congregational intolerance, to New Hampshire, and thence to Schenectady. Johnston's ordination they declared "disorderly" and burnt his church. But as that cause of Indian unrest promised settlement, grave disputes were rising among the whites themselves, the colonies against England, disputes about stamped paper and ancient rights and taxation without representation—matters that were utterly beyond the Indians' comprehension. They had been skilfully bound by Sir William in attachment to the King; their powder and ball, their blankets and hatchets, their gratuities of food against the bitter winter starvation, all came from the good King; and they were bewildered as they now saw a deepening revolt and hatred against this beneficent friend; the militiaman or rifle ranger carving on his powder horn the rude couplet, beneath some ruder caricature of Britain's monarch,

I, powder, and my brother, ball,
Foemen are to tyrants all.

But the quarrel grew, and the Indian could not fail to be involved in it. Hope of aid from him induced the Tories to tamper with his love of blood and plunder; the King's ministers even offered bounties for the scalps of rebels, $20.00 for a baby's scalp. Dread of him led the Colonials to cross measures; to coax him to take their side, to persuade him to stand aloof, yet to send one and another threatening expedition into his country prepared to treat with Brant, or capture him, burn his villages, destroy his crops of corn, beans and pumpkins, and cut down his apple trees. The Mohawks, after the battles of Concord and Lexington in 1775, were led to retire in a body to Canada, the exciting news of the Patriots' resistance being so made use of by Colonel Guy Johnson that the whole tribe regarded war as upon them.

They left their memorial in the name of the river, but it was an exile from which they were never to return. Indians were here and there shot or captured, and not seldom scalped; Tim. Murphy[2] boasted his record of forty Indians killed by his one hand. Finally the large mili-

---

2. The famous "Tim" Murphy boasted his record of forty (40) Indians killed by his own hand. The following story of him survives at Cherry Valley. On a geological shelf or terrace in the hills west of the village, there was a high level trail, by following which the savages could pass around unseen, meandering with the hills, but keeping above the houses. An Indian passing by on this track and seeing Murphy within hail conferring with Clyde and Wells, was tempted to call out an insulting challenge and passed on. The marksman knew that he would return, lay for him concealed, and shot him as he reached the spot where he had uttered the insult.

tary operations connected with the campaign against Burgoyne threw the savages over to the side of the king in hot anger and revenge. If a people do not take up war until passion is roused, this ingredient was now furnished.

The story of St. Leger's expedition to the Mohawk Valley from Oswego, the attempt on Fort Schuyler and the bloody ambuscade at Oriskany, is too long to be introduced here; but the awful slaughter inflicted on the Indians at Oriskany, especially the Senekees, while themselves inflicting an equal carnage upon the Provincials, sent them howling back to their villages and vowing desperate revenge for the loss of a hundred of their braves, and particularly against Cherry Valley, for when Herkimer was felled and Colonel Cox and many other officers slain at the outset, it was Colonel Campbell and Major Clyde, both Cherry Valley men, who directed the stubborn continuance of the fight and brought off the remnant of the force, retreating but substantially victorious.

That was in 1777. Burgoyne's grand scheme failed; invasion was averted from the rich grain lands of the Mohawk, and there seemed hope for the inhabitants of the frontier, where the Oneidas, at least, under the guidance of their missionary adviser, Mr. Kirkland, seemed not disposed to be unfriendly to the patriotic cause.

But the British in New Jersey had found Washington hard to handle, and in hope of weakening him Brant, the Butlers and other Royalist leaders on the border were directed to spread such alarm and create such distress and devastation as to draw away detachments for its relief.

A regiment under Colonel Ickabod Alden, the Sixth Masschusetts, made up in part of friends of the Cherry Valley people, but most inefficiently commanded, was at Albany, and in May started on its way to garrison the frontier posts. Schoharie was barely saved by the arrival of help in July; at Cobleskill, earlier, occurred a fight and defeat by Brant, in which Captain Patrick was killed, and German Flatts so late as September 17th was burnt, and yet before any aid reached it; so tardy was the action of Alden, as well as of the local military.

The main body of the regiment, 230 strong, with the lieutenant colonel, destined for Cherry Valley, only arrived July 24th, the colonel himself only on the 30th. Springfield had been burnt June 18th, and

124

a swarm of fleeing refugees from every quarter had brought the news of the shocking slaughter, on July 3rd, at Wyoming, and well-founded rumours of what was being planned against their own settlement. On remote farms the rapid-moving chief appeared, requiring every man to declare for the king or flee with wife and little ones. The hope of Brant would seem to have been, while guiding his tribes in a war in aid of the royal cause, to keep their savage impulses in check. Thus he burnt Springfield, but first gathered the women and children into a house to be saved. He burnt German Flatts, but the people had already taken refuge in the forts on the river.

Against Cherry Valley in particular he must have been reluctant to move, for the people were his personal friends. John Wells had been the respected associate of Sir William Johnson in public affairs at Johnstown, both, it is true, now dead, but the families still intimate. In the trench war Wells had built a fort at Oghwaga for the Indians, and he and Colonel Campbell had served as officers under Johnson at Fort Edward.

Mr. Dunlop had been in happier times an adviser and sharer with Brant in the missionary and civilizing projects which he had promoted. Colonel Clyde and his apprentice with Mr. Kirkland, about the year 1770, had erected a church for the Oneidas at their castle, an enterprise such as Brant assisted with warm approval and by raising money. Brant was a frequent visitor and old acquaintance of Mrs. Clyde's, who as Catherine Wasson, at Schenectady, had been the friend and playmate of the beautiful Lady of Johnson Hall, his sister, Mollie Brant. Even a man like Colonel John Butler, who commanded at Wyoming, said afterwards that he would have gone on his hands and knees to save the Wells family.

But society was cloven asunder, and in the unscrupulous Walter Butler, his son, and his crew of Tories, Brant was fated to co-operate with men that put all humane considerations at defiance. The spirit of the Indians was hard to control; his own Mohawks felt that their lands were gone forever; and the Tories, a bad lot generally, included every low renegade and every unmitigated brute on the border. The strife degenerated to utter butchery, and Brant must bear the odium. An incentive to rapine with such men, not often noticed, was the prospect of ransom for captives, women and children, and the sale of such slaves as could be raided away.

Mention is made in the list of captives of "Mr. Dunlop's negro wench" and other slaves, who were carried off, even when white captives were set free; and of these latter the families of men of importance were likely to be retained as prisoners in order to keep their husbands and fathers busy and anxious for their recovery, and so cripple their activity in the war.

It was a summer of terror. The large buildings of Colonel Campbell had been stockaded early in the year. General Lafayette at Johnstown advised the erection of a large fortification round the grave yard and commodious church. Early in June the people moved in here, with the fugitives from Springfield and nearby places, together with those from Unadilla under Rev. Mr. Johnston, who was made chaplain of the garrison, while his sons enlisted or scouted. All along urgent appeals and efforts had been made to secure defenders, with little success.

Of 600 militia summoned at Canajoharie only 200 responded. At Cherry Valley there were only 80 armed men in July, owing to the demands of the harvest and for the soldiers elsewhere. June 5 Clyde reports to General Stark, "from 600-700 cattle feeding within a circle of ¾ of a mile, and not over 30 men that would stand their ground if attacked."

He pleads for assistance to save these large supplies from being "lost to freedom." Yet Brant, spying from the overlooking Lady Hill, refrained from an attempt to surprise it with a small force he had, by mistaking a train of children playing soldier with sticks on the green before Colonel Campbell's house, for a body of troops. It, was in seeking to waylay a messenger who might explain this mysterious force that his own valued friend, Lieutenant Wormuth, or Wormwood, of Palatine, on his return from announcing the actual approach of a few militiamen under Colonel Ford, was shot at "Wormwood rock" in the ravine of Teckaharawa.

The rock is still pointed out, called Brant's Rock, from behind which the Indian who was with him rashly and against his orders shot down his boyhood neighbour as he rode by on his horse, his orderly making his escape to carry the news of the tragedy to the friends of both men; for Brant's ancestral home was at Canajoharie.

Cherry Valley[3] in the forty years since its settlement had grown to be a place of some sixty families, including some exceptionally intelligent and prominent persons. Judge John Wells had died, but Mr. Dunlop was still living, and the Wells homestead was occupied by the large family of Robert Wells. Captain Robert McKean, an intrepid Indian fighter, was active with a body of rangers scouting everywhere, gathering information and watching the movements of the foe. The important family of the Harpers had lately moved to the Charlotte Valley, but operated their mill at the Beaver Dam to furnish lumber for completing the redouts. Colonel Campbell we have seen at the Battle of Oriskany[4]; and among those most to be relied upon was Samuel Clyde, a veteran of the earlier wars; bred a ship carpenter, he had built naval docks at Halifax and *batteaux* for the expedition to Ticonderoga, and had fought at Frontenac. At Schenectady he had married his brave wife, a woman of superior mind, a niece of Matthew Thornton, the patriot leader of New Hampshire and signer of the Declaration of Independence.

The emphatic choice of the patriot cause by the people of Cherry Valley had been publicly declared as early as 1775. A liberty meeting was held in the church to express sympathy with the people of Boston, and to ratify the acts of the Continental Congress. They denounced the attempts of the Tories at Johnstown through the Grand Jury to commit Tryon County to the Royalist cause. The strong Whig sentiments of the place, against the plans of the Johnsons and Colo-

3. Halsey. The reason assigned by Col. Johnson for the building of this fort was that "the fort at Cherry Valley was too far distant;" implying the existence of such a stronghold there at the time of the French War. It would naturally be a stockade enclosing the house and premises of Wells himself on the hill, and doubtless included the shelter of the log church which tradition locates on that hill near the Wells house. There is no local recollection of such a fort, but at the very first there must have been a protection against surprise and treachery such as a fortified house. The good terms on which the people at Cherry Valley lived with the Indians caused all trace of both these forts to disappear very soon. A body of 800 men was raised at Canajoharie in the French War and 100 of them were sent to Cherry Valley.
The need of a fort at Oghwaga for the Indians was the direct result of Braddock's defeat, which threatened to carry the Indians of Pennsylvania and the Western New York tribes over to the French, since they seemed to be more powerful than the English. Pontiac's war, in 1763-4, and the resulting disturbance and famine, broke up the Mission at Oghwaga, the school being removed to the foot of Otsego Lake, where it would be within easy reach at Cherry Valley.
4. *The Battle of Oriskany 1777* by Ellis H. Roberts also published by Leonaur.

nel Butler's Highlanders, were voiced in fiery speeches from Thomas Spencer, an Indian interpreter of rude eloquence, and from Mr. John Moore, a man of ability and education Delegate from Tryon County in the Provincial Congress, but incapacitated for war service by a lameness. He with Campbell and Clyde were on the Committee of Safety for Palatine district, and two others, James Willson and Hugh Mitchell, served later on the Schenectady Committee. A letter from these earnest men to the committee at Albany, imploring help to save the frontier, concludes as follows:

> In a word, gentlemen, it is our fixed resolution to support and carry into execution everything recommended by the Continental Congress, and to be free or die.

Yet their sobriety and firm religious principle are attested as well by a letter to the Palatine Committee objecting to a meeting needlessly called on a Sunday:

> For unless the necessity of the committee sitting super-exceed the duties to be performed in attending the public worship of God, we think it ought to be put off till another day.

Sir William Johnson had died in 1774. The truculent Toryism of Guy Johnson, his successor, aroused deep hostility, which led him either to feel or feign fear for his own safety. He declared that he was in danger of capture by the "Bostonians," and with the body of Mohawks retired, first to Fort Stanwix, and finally to Montreal. He here co-operated with Sir Guy Carlton in fomenting the hatred of the Cayugas and Senecas. From Canada round by the lakes and forests, and up the Susquehanna to Oghwaga and Unadilla, where Brant had his rendezvous in the rear of Cherry Valley, trickled mingling rivulets, red coats, green-clad riflemen and Canadian half-breeds, Tories and malcontents, and gathering bands of stealthy Indians, driving out all who would not declare for King George, and concentrating a force of 1,500 to 2,000 men. Along the flats of the streams, under British incitement, wide fields of corn and vegetables were planted for feeding them.

Yet the summer passed away and no attempt had been made on Cherry Valley. Colonel Alden, an eastern man unused to Indian ways, could not realize the danger, notwithstanding the scenes going on around him, and the serious advice of citizens of experience. "The depredations were from small bands; he would send out and arrest them." His theory was that savages would never stand against disciplined soldiers; besides, they had artillery, two swivel guns. The families in the fort were not allowed to remain; instead, he quartered his officers in their houses, himself with his lieutenant colonel fixing his headquarters at that of Robert Wells, a quarter of a mile from the fort. There is marrying and giving in marriage, nevertheless, as well as eating and much drinking, in the midst of warlike alarms. Lieutenant McKendry in his Journal records, September 9, Captain McKean returned from a scout to Unadilla with two prisoners, and October 22 is present at the captain's marriage to Mrs. Jenny Campbell.

The day following he is at the wedding of Sergeant Elijah Dickerman and Letty Gibbons. "Drank 7 Galls, wine." Lieutenant Colonel Stacy and Captain Ballard have a horse race and Stacy wins the bet. Viewing some horses at John Campbell's he "drinks cyder," and "milk punch" at Mr. Ramsie's with Captain Parker; milk punch also at Alden's headquarters "when Fort Alden is named by Capt. Hickling." He goes "to Harmony Hall and drank some Grog," and goes to Harmony Hall again some days later, what for not said, but presumably same refreshment. October 15 he "wet his appointment," "wine 28 dollars," and Lieutenant William White wets his, "Wine Amt. 36 dollars." Surely our liberties were achieved not without mighty wrestling with the liquor interest. But they were all in it. The very first day of his arrival he records apparently a visit of courtesy upon a family friend of other days. "Went to Rev'd Mr. Dunlop's & drank sillabub while discoursing the old Gentleman about sundries affairs."

Brant meanwhile ceases his activities not a moment. His design may perhaps have been by repeated alarms and threats to frighten his friends in the place into taking flight, and then to attack the stockade, a measure of legitimate war. But two things conspired to defeat such a design, if he entertained it; in the first place many of the people did flee, as did Mr. Dunlop, removing to Albany the best of his goods. But September and October passed, and winter beginning with November in that elevated climate, they came back, partly to care for their stock, partly thinking the danger was passed from the lateness of the season. So that when the blow came it was far more calamitous than the Indian leader expected it to be.

In the second place, his own situation was affected by a blow dealt him from Schoharie under orders from the energetic Governor Clinton. There was a patriot Colonel Butler there, William, who with great speed crossed his regiment from the Schoharie through the forest to the Delaware, and thence down the Owleout to the Susquehanna, and on a rapid sweep uprooted both Unadilla and Oghwaga; a stroke which had it been accomplished earlier might have saved the whole frontier. Brant gave up the contest for the season and was on his way to Niagara to winter, but at Tioga Point he met Walter Butler with his motley force wild with the project of an attack on Cherry Valley. Brant was reluctant to return, reluctant to serve under Butler, whom he despised.

Perhaps he hoped by being present to guide counsels and mitigate some features of the stroke, from which everything was to be feared. At all events he consented to join the enterprise. There was a disused trail, midway, neglected by the scouts sent out south and west; by this they stole around the hills, delayed by bad weather, yet undiscovered, till they reached the rear of the settlement after daylight on the 11th of November. A notification from Colonel Gansevoort at Fort Schuyler had told of the meeting of Butler and Brant at Tioga and of their starting for Cherry Valley. But the pickets were merely dispatched along the usual roads, the feeble scouts were captured, the onset had all the advantage of a surprise, and the incredulous Alden at the Wells house was caught before he could reach the fort. They numbered about 800 men, of whom 30 were British troops under four officers, 600 Indians, principally Senecas under the bitterly cruel Hiokatoo (whose wife was widely known as Mary Jamieson), and 150 Tories, many in Indian paint and of worse than Indian atrocity.

The wakeful Mrs. Clyde had dreamed of Indian alarms and of warnings from Mollie Brant, and at daylight urged her husband to repair to the fort and learn if all were right. He had not time to return when a wounded rider came in with the word that the foe had overtaken and shot him. The signal gun was fired, a dismal rainy morning. Mrs. Clyde being prepared, gathered her family and fled to the ravine as the savages emerged from the forest behind. There were eight children besides an apprentice and a little dog. The babe never wailed, the dog did not bark. The rain turned to sleet and snow, yet all escaped after a night's exposure and terror, a relief party coming out from the fort and all running the gauntlet of the enemy's fire in crossing the open ground in front of the palisade. A battle raged here for hours, renewed on the 12th, but the cannon compelled the foe to retire. Colonel Clyde was luckily within, and he seems to have assumed the command, or it might have been taken, as nearly all its officers were surprised at their quarters in the houses of the settlement.

The Wells house had been the first to be attacked. They were at worship when the rifle of a Tory felled the head of the household. The whole family were slain, Robert Wells, his wife and four children, his mother, brother and sister and three domestics, together with the guard of Colonel Alden. Having secured the Lieutenant Colonel, Stacy, Brant demanded, "Who runs there?" and being told, "The colonel," he turned over his prisoner and pursued the fugitive, calling on him to surrender. Alden turned to use his pistol, but the tomahawk flew and he fell in the roadway. The body, dragged to one side, was found on a spot still pointed out just below the ascent to the Wells house. This is the account given in a MS. by Judge George C. Clyde, and the account also related to me personally by Mr. George Ripley, both of them grandsons of Colonel Clyde; namely that Colonel Alden was killed by Brant himself, but, as he alleged, in self-defence. A pillar of concrete with marble tablet erected on this spot marks the occurrence.

Every foot of the Cherry Valley soil has its tale of the experiences of that day. Hugh Mitchell avoided the Indians, but gained his house to find his wife and four children left for dead, two being carried captives. One child showed signs of life, and as he was in the act of restoring her the blow of a Tory extinguished the spark; all that was left was to load the corpses on a sled, and over the fresh fallen snow, bring and lay them with the ghastly rows with which the great trench was being filled. He recognized his near neighbour, a Royalist renegade named Newbury, as the man who committed this brutal act, and he had the satisfaction, later, of bringing him to the gallows for his crime. Mitchell lies buried at Cherry Valley at the age of 102 years.

Mrs. Elizabeth Dickson escaped with her children to the hill behind the house, but her infant fretting she ventured back for milk and did not return. The daughter, Eleanor, peering about, at length saw a scalpstick on which, drying, among others waved a tress of brilliant auburn of a colour such as there was none other in the settlement but her mother's. The Campbell home was defended so valiantly by the aged Captain Cannon, the grandfather, a naval veteran, that the Indians let him go; but his wife was captured, and, too feeble to make the journey, was struck down in the snow by an Indian the next day, and her body was buried at the fort.

It may have been this piece of barbarity which led Brant to insist on the release of the majority of the women and children. Forty-five of these were now permitted to return. The thirty-four carried off, as reported in a return by Colonel Harper shortly after, included all males captured and the families of prominent persons, and likewise some eight or ten negroes. Thirty-three inhabitants were massacred and fourteen of the regiment, besides the colonel. Colonel Campbell was absent at the time; his wife was captured with her infant and other children, except one, William, rescued and carried to the river by a faithful slave. He was afterwards Surveyor General of the state.

Mrs. Campbell's experience was most harrowing. The murdered Mrs. Cannon was her mother. With the little babe in her arms she made the bitter journey all the way down the Susquehanna to Tioga Point, and up the Chemung to the Seneca Castle. Here she passed the winter, not ill-treated by the Indians, but destitute of sufficient clothing and in deepest anxiety about her children's fate as well as of her friends. One day a squaw asked her why she wore the linen cap, then the mark of a lady, saying she had such a cap, and produced it. Mrs. Campbell recognized it as the one worn by her loved friend, Jane Wells! Towards spring the British officers at Fort Niagara, hearing that there was a lady who was a prisoner at the castle, sent a messenger on horseback with a supply of female raiment and provisions for her relief.

As soon as the season permitted she was carried to Fort Niagara and by the officers ransomed from the Indians, she returning the kindness by services with her needle, until she was sent to Montreal. After nearly two years of captivity she was exchanged for a Mrs. Butler and her children. In the cartel boat on Lake Champlain she was accompanied by several young ladies who had been at school at Montreal and were detained by the hostilities till this opportunity of a return, and after being fired upon and landed in the wilds of Vermont, owing to a false alarm, they all reached their friends in Albany.

Two of the Campbell boys were lost among the Indians and adopted by them. Matthew returned adorned with ornaments of silver and diamonds, doubtless rifled from the body of some slain officer. The Indians had adopted him as a chief, and treated him with honour. The other son, James, six years old, was lost for some three years, forgetting his small knowledge of the English speech. Shortly after his restoration occurred the tour of General Washington over this frontier, who being entertained at Colonel Campbell's house, held this interesting child upon his knee. He lived to be ninety-eight, when the present writer attended his funeral in 1870. After the Civil war he was taken to Albany and shook the hand of General Grant. He was the father of the author of the Annals of Tryon County, and grandfather of Douglas Campbell who wrote *The Puritan in Holland, England and America.*

The Massachusetts troops passed the winter in the fort, and in June following joined the expedition under General Sullivan at Otsego Lake. The fort was dismantled and the church eventually burnt, as were practically all the buildings of the place. Four years later, on the 18th of April, 1781, a second descent was made on the few venturesome people who had returned to Cherry Valley, by a band of eighty men, who killed eight persons and took fourteen prisoners. Till that year Captain McKean had been as ever active, but that summer Colonel Willett with 150 Americans fought a battle with from 200 to 300 Indians at Durlagh (Torlock), some miles east of Cherry Valley, winning a fine victory, but the brave captain was carried off by his men wounded to his death.

When Mr. Dunlop returned from Albany that Autumn to see to his affaire for the winter, together with his wife and daughter (unmarried) he was accompanied by his married daughter, Mrs. Eleanor Willson, and by a young man to whom Elizabeth expected to be married. This young man was killed. Elizabeth passed the later years of her life at Bernardsville, N. J., in the home of her niece, Mrs. Dr. Boyland, and as "Aunt Whitie" was well remembered by her great niece, who died at over ninety, a year ago, the mother of Bishop Fitzgerald of the Methodist Episcopal Church. The effects saved from Cherry Valley were burnt in a fire at Barnardsville, and Mrs. Fitzgerald related that the daughter of Mr. Dunlop used to say that her greatest regret in this fire was not the household articles so much as the loss of the family coat of arms, the mark of their respectable standing. The arms of the Dunlops forms an adornment of the tablet set up in the Cherry Valley Church.

Mrs. Dunlop at the moment of the alarm happened to have in her arms the child of the negro slave woman. When they said the barn was on fire she stepped to the door to look and was shot by a bullet from an unseen hand. In the rush that followed some unfeeling brute severed the arm that held the child and flung it into an apple tree that stood long after nearby. Violence to Mr. Dunlop was averted for a moment by the astonishment of the Indian who would have scalped him at seeing come off in his hand the wig which he wore as a gentlemen of position; when a chief named Little Aaron interposed to save the venerable pastor, shocked and prostrated already almost to his death by the awful scenes that were to end his peaceful labours. He and his unmarried daughter were prisoners, but were soon released and made their way with the wretched train of some 200 others that were reported by Colonel Clyde as rendered destitute by the calamity. He soon died, probably at Schenectady, but where his ashes repose is not known.

His little grandson, John Wells, was the only member of that family who survived that day. Mrs. Willson just before the massacre besought her sister, Mary Wells, to allow her to take this child with her back to Schenectady, where he had shown great aptitude in a few weeks' schooling he had enjoyed that summer, and she left Cherry Valley with some officers a day or so before the attack. He lived to graduate at Princeton and to become the most eminent lawyer in New York City. As a young man he co-operated with Alexander Hamilton in the publication of the *Federalist* newspaper, and some of the pieces in it attributed to the older hands were said to be from his pen. At his untimely death from yellow fever, in 1832, a bust of his beautiful head was placed in old Grace Church, with this inscription:

Erected by the Bar of New York as a tribute of their respect for the memory of John Wells, who adorned their profession by his integrity, eloquence and learning.

This monument is now one of the most beautiful adornments of St. Paul's Chapel in Broadway.

One of the most vividly lifelike accounts of the experiences and privations of those who escaped the hands of the Indians at the time of the massacre, as well as a most interesting sketch of the difficulties and hardships of the immigrants in the period of poverty previous to the war, is given from the life of one who survived them, in *Jane Ferguson's Narrative*, who in extreme age, but in a most intelligent manner, dictated the tale of her people's settlement a few miles west of Cherry Valley, now Springfield, a number of years before the war of the Revolution, of their retreat to the neighbourhood of Schenectady, their starving life through the years of strife, and the bitter struggles of the return. It is too long to be quoted here and would lose its interest in an abridgement. It was published in the American Monthly Magazine of the D. A. R.

Immediately upon the close of the war the Cherry Valley people returned to rebuild their homes. The ancient trustee's book of the Church bears on its first page, in a hand writing like a piece of fine engraving, the quaint record of a gathering at the ruins of their sanctuary among the graves of their kindred and hard by the trench where the victims of the fatal day were buried. "We the ancient inhabitants of Cherry Valley, having returned from exile, finding ourselves destitute of our church officers, to wit, elders and deacons:—our legislature having enacted a law for the relief of those, etc."—they proceeded to appoint a day for the rehabilitation of their Zion.

The rude and simple edifice was built, but it was not till 1796, eighteen years after the cessation of Mr. Dunlop's labours, that a pastor could be secured in a young man of talent, who with the pulpit assumed charge of the Academy, then just chartered under the newly founded Regents of the University. A marble tablet was erected in the church, in 1904, the gift of a grandson of this young divine and teacher, the Right Reverend Henry C. Potter, Bishop of New York. It reads as follows:

The Reverend Eliphalet Nott; D. D. LL. D.
Clarum Et Venerabile Nomen,
for sixty-one years President of Union College,
was from 1796 till 1798

135

Minister of this Church and in the Academy here
began his career as
EDUCATOR.

There is also in the church a memorial brass to Judge William W. Campbell, referred to above as the author of a very early book upon the history of this frontier, to which every writer on the subject must ever be indebted, *The Annals of Tryon County, or the Border Warfare of New York*. He is commemorated as *Vir bonus, Judex Justus, Institutionum Amicus*.

The writer acknowledges the help derived at many points from *The Old New York Frontier* by Francis W. Halsey, the best treatment of the general subject yet written.

Wyoming Valley a Sketch of Its Early Annals

Isaac A. Chapman

Contents

Wyoming Valley

Wyoming is the final corruption of *Maughwa-wame*, signifying, in the dialect of the Delaware Indians, "large flats without trees"—in the "Mingo" or Iroquois dialect, *Sgahontowanno*, meaning the same.

Indian traditions make the ancestors of the "Delawares" to have come from the Northwest. They displaced the "Allegenni," whom they found in possession, and occupied the country from the Hudson to the Potomac. The "Shawanese" came from the South, settled on the Wabash River, and subsequently divided, part remaining there and part coming to Wyoming. The "Nanticokes" came from Maryland and settled in the lower end of the valley. These tribes all willingly or unwillingly acknowledged the dominion of the Six Nations, or confederacy of New York Indians which embraced the Oneidas, Oaondagas, Senecas, Cayugas, Mohawks and Tuscaroras.

When William Penn purchased the Delaware title to the lands below the Kitatiany or Blue Mountain, he made inquiry after other titles and subsequently learned that the Six Nations claimed them. A council was therefore called, which met at Philadelphia in 1742. The result of this council was the expulsion of the Delawares from the country below the mountains and their settlement in and about Wyoming.

Soon after this event the "Grasshopper War" broke out between the Shawanese and the Delawares. This resulted in the expulsion of the former from the Valley, leaving the Delawares in possession.

The French having built a chain of fortresses along the western frontier, succeeded in winning to their interests the Shawanese and Delawares. This led to a council at Easton, in which a treaty of peace was concluded between the Governor of Pennsylvania, on the one hand, and Tedeuscund, *sachem* of the Delawares, on the other. Subsequently, another grand council was held at the same place, in which all the Indian tribes of New York and Pennsylvania were represented, and the peace was confirmed by a general treaty in the year 1753.

After this brief review of Indian history of Wyoming, we now come to its "white" history. To understand this, it is necessary to glance at the several charters from the British Crown.

March 3, 1620, King James I. gave a charter, called the Plymouth Charter, embracing the territory in America between the fortieth and forty-eighth parallels of north latitude, and running through to the South Sea or Pacific Ocean. The Plymouth Company conveyed their rights to the Duke of Warwick, who in turn transferred them to Lords Say, Seal and Brook, in 1631. Under these noblemen Connecticut was settled, and the Colony acquired the title in 1644. The Dutch, however, had discovered the Hudson River, and taken possession of the adjacent territory, as far up as Albany, in 1614. The General Court at Hartford now addressed a petition to the king, and on the 23rd of April, 1662, His Majesty granted a charter to the colony of Connecticut, embracing "all the territory bounded north by the south line of Massachusetts, south by the sea, and running on the line of the Massachusetts Colony to the South Sea."

March 12, 1664, King Charles II. granted a patent to the Duke of York, and on November 28, 1683, a mutual survey, jointly made by the Colony of Connecticut and the province of New York, and confirmed by both parties (24th February 1685,) fixed the western boundary of Connecticut at a point twenty miles east of the Hudson River. Thus it will be seen that the Connecticut Charter, two years older than the Duke of York's, embraced the territory between the present parallels of Connecticut, continued through the country "to the South Sea," saving and reserving the Dutch settlements which had been expected in the purchase from the Plymouth Company. March 4, 1681, King Charles II. granted a charter to William Penn for territory "from a point on the Delaware River, twelve miles north of New Castle, unto the three-and-fortieth degree of north latitude, and extending westward five degrees in longitude from the said eastward bounds." This charter overlapped the north bounded of Connecticut and embraced Wyoming, thus establishing two conflicting claims, under European titles, but, as yet, neither party having extinguished the Indian title.

Observe that the modes of acquiring and possessing new lands, under the charters of Connecticut and Pennsylvania, were essentially different. In Pennsylvania the lands were all granted to one individual, and he possessed the exclusive right of purchasing of the Indians. In the Connecticut Charter the lands were granted to the inhabitants of the colony in their collective capacity, and all possessed an equal right to purchase. In Pennsylvania, claimants held of the "Proprietaries." In Connecticut, individuals or companies, and generally some religious corporation, took possession, purchased the Indian title, and then settled by townships.

During the year 1753 a number of Connecticut people associated themselves together as the Susquehanna Company, for the purpose of purchasing lands of the Indians and forming settlements at Wyoming. James Hamilton, Proprietary Governor of the Province of Pennsylvania, at once wrote to Sir William Johnson, His Majesty's Indian Agent for the Colonies, desiring his good offices to prevent a purchase of the Indians by the Susquehanna Company at the approaching council to be held at Albany.

The agents of the Susquehanna Company, however, appeared at Albany and effected a purchase July 11, 1754. This purchase included Wyoming, and embraced the territory as far west as the heads of the Allegheny River. The commissioners of Pennsylvania to the Albany Council had many conferences with the Indians while there, a report of which conferences is entered on the minutes of council at Philadelphia, Aug. 6, 1754, as follows:

> The commissioners of Pennsylvania, having a private treaty with the Six Nations while at Albany, for the purpose of buying lands, their report was likewise read and ordered to be entered.

The Susquehanna Company at this time consisted of 673 persons, ten of whom lived in Pennsylvania, and they proposed at once to divide up the purchase among the claimants.

The treaty at Albany above referred to, as concluded with the Six Nations by Pennsylvania, was—

> . . . . for all the said River Susquehanna, and on both sides thereof, eastward as far as the springs thereof, and westward to the setting sun, and from the mouth of said river up to Tayamantesatche or the Blue Mountain.

This deed was signed by twenty-three chiefs of the Oneidas, Onondagas, Senecas and Tuscaroras. The purchase did not, however, include Wyoming, which they utterly refused to sell.

In August, 1762, about two hundred persons left Connecticut, and, under the authority of the Susquehanna Company, commenced a settlement at Wyoming, building their block house and cabins at the mouth of Mill Creek, where that stream is now spanned by the aqueduct of the Pennsylvania canal.

The Proprietaries of Pennsylvania about this time submitted their claims to the judgement of the English Attorney General. This functionary (afterwards Lord Camden) replied, taking grounds in their favour, and assuming that the settlement of Connecticut's boundaries with New York barred all claim west of the line thereby drawn parallel to the Hudson River and twenty miles east of it.

The government of Connecticut now proceeded to submit their claims to eminent counsel in England, who decided "that the agreement between Connecticut and New York as to their mutual boundaries could in no wise affect any claims which either party might have in other quarters, and as the charter to Connecticut ante-dated that to William Penn by eighteen years, the Crown could make no effectual grant of a territory so recently granted to others."

Hitherto the surrounding Indians had acted in a friendly manner, but now a change was to come. Tedeuscund, the great Delaware *Sachem*, was about this time murdered by a party of the Six Nations, in revenge for his assumed superiority at the Great Council in 1758, and, with Indian cunning, this deed of treachery was charged upon the whites.

The consequences were soon apparent. On the 16th of October, 1763, while busy in the fields, the settlers were attacked, twenty killed and the village burned. The survivors—men, women and children—fled to the mountains, and in their nakedness and distress commenced a sad journey of two hundred and fifty miles on foot to Connecticut.

Peace between England and France having this year been concluded, the government of the former instructed its agents to cultivate peace with the Indians.

Accordingly a general treaty was concluded with them at Fort Stanwix, in October, 1768, at which the Proprietaries of Pennsylvania procured a deed from the Six Nations for all the lands within the province of Pennsylvania not hitherto sold. This purchase included Wyoming and all the territory previously sold to the Susquehanna Company.

A meeting of that company was now called, and it was resolved that "forty persons at once proceed to Wyoming and commence settlement *as proprietors*, to be followed by two hundred more in the Spring, and that £200 be raised to supply them with implements and necessaries." The resolution also designated Isaac Tripp, Benjamin Follett, John Jenkins, Wm. Buck and Benj. Shoemaker a special committee to supervise the government and superintendence of the colony. This Committee were to be increased to nine men on the arrival of the Spring reinforcements, and the Committee, as thus constituted, were clothed with full executive, legislative and judicial powers, subject, however (as in the Spartan government of Lycurgus), to the supreme authority of the Company, which was to be exercised at Hartford.

Alarmed at these energetic movements, which evidently "meant business," the Proprietaries, of Pennsylvania, acting by John Penn, leased to Charles Stewart, Amos Ogden and John Jennings, one hundred acres of land at Wyoming, "for seven years with authority to establish a trading post, and to defend it and those claiming under them from all enemies whatsoever."

Stewart at once proceeded to lay out the valley into two manors— one on the east side of the Susquehanna, extending from Nanticoke, to Monockonock Island, to be called "Manor of Stoke," and the other on the west side, of the same dimensions, to be called "Manor of Sunbury." The Pennsylvania party took possession of the improvements from which the Indians had driven the Connecticut men, and commenced new improvements at the same point in January, 1769.

On the eighth of the following month, the "forty" Connecticut men arrived and found Stewart and Ogden in possession of a fortified block house at Mill Creek. The Connecticut party at once besieged the block house. After some time, a parley took place, during which Jennings, by stratagem, captured three of the principal men of the Yankees, and took them to Easton. They were, however, soon released on bail, returned to Wyoming, and, with their companions, proceeded to erect a substantial stockade, surrounded by rampart and entrenchment, calling it "Fort Durkee."

Jennings assembled a large party of Pennsylvania men, and arrived at Wyoming about the last of May, 1769, but found the Connecticut people too well prepared to venture an attack. Thus, ready for coming events, the latter began their agricultural operations for the season. The Susquehanna Company now despatched Col. Dyer and Major Elderkin to Philadelphia, and laid before Benjamin Chew, Esq., agent for the Proprietaries, a proposition "to settle all disputes by a court of law to be constituted by the parties, or by referees mutually chosen, whose decisions should be conclusive." This proposition was rejected, as military preparations were now on foot for the reduction of the Connecticut settlement.

A formal letter of instructions was made out by the Pennsylvania government, and directed to the Sheriff of Northampton county, directing him to raise the posse of the county, proceed to Wyoming and dispossess all persons holding any other title than that of the Proprietaries.

Amos Ogden, with a party of forty men, hearing of Jennings' approach, surprised and captured several of the yankee families, among whom was that of Col Durkee. Jennings arrived before the fort with two hundred men and a four-pounder cannon, and proceeded to reduce it. This was effected in a few days.

By the articles of capitulation the fort and buildings were to be given up to Ogden and Jennings, it being promised that the property, homes and crops should be unhurt, and should be guarded by seventeen of the Connecticut men, left for that purpose.

As soon as the surrender was complete, the Pennsylvanians commenced an indiscriminate plunder of everything valuable, driving off the cattle and swine towards the Delaware and the seventeen men left in possession fled for their lives, leaving their foes in undisputed mastery.

In February, 1770, a number of Lancaster countymen, sympathizing with the Connecticut settlers, came up to the valley. These were commanded by Lazarus Stewart, and were joined by a few of the returned settlers. They invested Fort Durkee, and captured it with little opposition. They now proceeded to the reduction of Ogden's block house, and for that purpose erected another immediately opposite it on the west side of the river, mounting the four-pounder as a siege gun.

Finding the range too great, they transported their artillery again to the east side, threw up a breastwork, and soon succeeded in burning the attached storehouse and capturing the garrison of the block house, Ogden and his party were allowed to depart, leaving six occupants in one house to take charge of the effects of the Pennsylvanians.

Governor Penn and the Proprietaries now proceeded to raise a force of over one hundred and sixty men, which was placed under Ogden's command, and they, in company with Aaron Van Campen and other civil officers representing the State authority, marched upon the Valley.

From the summit of "Penobscot" this party reconnoitred the flats, saw the settlers disperse to their labours on the morning of Sept. 22, 1770, and at once made such disposition as enabled them to capture

OLD FORTY FORT

the whole Connecticut party, who were marched to Easton jail, while Ogden and his men proceeded to gather the harvest and plunder the settlement of everything movable.

The Connecticut settlers having now about disappeared from the disputed territory, the Pennsylvanians garrisoned the fort and considered themselves secure for the winter.

Delusive hope! On the morning of December 18th, at three o'clock, a "huzza for King George!" was heard within the stockade, and the garrison awaking found Stewart with thirty men in complete possession. These immediately drove the Pennsylvanians to the mountains, and again garrisoned and victualled the fort for another struggle.

The Judges of the Supreme Court of Pennsylvania now issued warrants for the arrest of Lazarus Stewart and his companions, directed to the sheriff of Northampton county. He raised a posse, and arriving at Wyoming on the 18th day of January, 1771, demanded admittance into the fort.

Stewart, looking over the parapet, informed him that none but friends could be admitted; that Wyoming was under the jurisdiction of Connecticut, and that no authority emanating from Pennsylvania could be recognized.

The sheriff's party then fired upon the fort, and the fire was instantly returned, killing Nathan Ogden, a brother of the Pennsylvania leader, Stewart that night abandoned the fort to the possession of twelve of his own men. These were captured and marched to Easton, leaving the fort in possession of Ogden.

About the 6th of July, Capt. Zebulon Butler, with seventy Connecticut men, arrived, and were soon after joined by Capt, Lazarus Stewart with a reinforcement. Ogden's party, which, with women and children, now amounted to eighty-two, occupied a new fort which they had built upon the river bank a short distance above Fort Durkee and named "Fort Wyoming," The Connecticut men at once threw up redoubts on both sides of the river, above and below the fort, and a third on a small hill adjacent, still known as "Redoubt Hill," thus completing the investment.

Ogden was equal to the emergency. On a moonlight night he tied his clothes in a bundle, surmounted it with his hat, and attaching a cord, permitted the bundle to float behind him while he swam down the river. Thus drawing the besieger's fire, he escaped, arrived safe at Philadelphia, and soon obtained assistance for further enterprises.

The council at once resolved that one hundred men should be raised for the relief of Wyoming and voted £300 expense money. This force was in two divisions, one commanded by Captain Joseph Morris, the other by Captain John Dick, and all under command of Col. Asher Clayton. But these were ambushed by the besiegers, and dispersed with the loss of four pack horses loaded with provisions, twenty-two men only succeeding in their attempt to enter the fort.

The siege was now pushed with all diligence, and on the 14th of August the fort surrendered, Clayton, Ogden and the Pennsylvanians agreeing to remove from the valley.

The government of Pennsylvania, finding that the Connecticut people had strongly fortified themselves, and that their number was rapidly increasing, gave orders for withdrawing the troops, and left the settlers in quiet possession.

Again this beautiful Valley enjoyed a short respite of repose and peace, which was improved in the most effective manner. They laid out townships, formed settlements, erected fortifications, levied and collected taxes, passed laws for the direction of civil suits, and established a militia.

Neither Greece nor Rome, in their happiest days, could boast a government more purely democratic. The meeting of the Proprietors formed the Grand Council, to which an appeal was in all cases reserved. Its records formed the Statute Book of the infant colony. The executive power vested in a committee of settlers, one from each township, deciding upon all matters civil and criminal. The judicial power inhered in the above bodies, and a third, or "Ordinary Court," consisting of three freeholders, who were to decide all questions arising between two or more individuals and make return to the "Committee of Settlers," who issued execution to the proper constable. Such was the simple and effectual scheme of government "for the well ordering and governing the proprietors and settlers on the Susquehanna Purchase."

[The author here remarks:—Several of the laws passed at this time have the appearance o great severity, but may have been justified by the circumstances of the times. One, in particular, passed at Wilkes-Barre, December 28th, 1772, provided " that no person or persons, settlers or foreigners, shall sell or give to any Indian any spirituous liquors on pain of forfeiture of all goods and chattels, rights and effects within this purchase, and

149

also be voted out of the company." Allow us to inquire *en passant* how much has the lapse of one hundred and six years enabled the children to improve on the legislation of the fathers?]

The General Assembly of Connecticut now passed an act creating a Board of Commissioners, with full power to make final settlement of all boundaries and claims in dispute. Accordingly, Col. Dyer, Dr. Johnson and Mr. Strong were commissioned, and in December, 1773, laid their case before the Council of Pennsylvania, at Philadelphia, reciting in full the boundaries described in the Connecticut charter of 1662, and adding, "which limits and boundaries do include a considerable part of the land afterwards granted by the Crown to Sir William Penn, in 1081, and which constitute a part of the Province of Pennsylvania, as now claimed by the Proprietaries," also adding, "and we, on the part of the said colony, are now ready to agree on Commissioners to run the lines of the patent, and execute the same in the most effective manner."

Governor Penn, in his reply of December 17th, declined to enter into any negotiations on the subject, declined to join in an application to His Majesty for the appointment of commissioners to settle the matter, and contented himself with the expression of an opinion that "the claim made by your government of any lands westward of New York is without the least foundation."

Much correspondence subsequently passed between the commissioners and the governor, eliciting, however, no new facts or principles. Among these letters was one from the governor, which laid stress upon the purchase made of the Indians at Fort Stanwix, in 1768. To this the commissioners reply:—

It were easy to observe that the purchase from the Indians by the Proprietaries, and the sales by them made, were they even more ancient than they are, could add no strength to the Pennsylvania title, since the right of pre-emption from the: natives was by the royal grant exclusively vested in the Colony of Connecticut.

On the 17th of January, 1774, the General Assembly of Pennsylvania addressed the governor, earnestly requesting him " to use every effort to call the claimants before His Majesty in Council, and bring the claim to an immediate decision," but the King of England had by this time more important matters to settle with his American subjects.

The colonists now abandoned the hope of being constituted a

separate colony by royal grant, and applied to the General Assembly of Connecticut for closer political annexation. An Act was accordingly passed in January, 1774, by which the Susquehanna settlements, bounded north and south by the charter limits, and extending fifteen miles beyond Wyoming, were constituted the "Town of Westmoreland," and attached to the county of Litchfield. From this date Wyoming ceased to exist as a separate "Republic," the laws of Connecticut being extended over her in full force.

These proceedings having been formally communicated to Governor Penn, he issued his proclamation forbidding all persons from attending " the Town Meeting thus notified by Zebulon Butler, and from settling any lands at Wyoming without consent of the Proprietaries." This proclamation appears to have been regarded by the inhabitants of the "Town of Westmoreland" with as little attention as they would a royal edict from the King of Spain.

A Yankee settlement commenced on the West Branch at Muncy, was attacked Sept 28th, 1775, by militia from Northumberland—part dispersed and part conveyed prisoners to Sunbury. Boats from Wyoming trading down the river were also waylaid and plundered near the later place.

Alarmed by the rekindling of civil war, at a time so inopportune, Congress at Philadelphia, resolved "that the Assemblies of the said colonies be requested to take the most effectual steps to prevent such hostilities."

No orders, however, came from any quarter's for the release of the prisoners at Sunbury, and the inhabitants of that good town became alarmed lest a detachment from Wyoming should descend the river for their rescue.

Wm. Plunkett, who had been a principal sharer in the booty obtained by pillage on the West Branch, joined with others in an address to the governor of Pennsylvania, setting forth the rapid growth of the yankee settlements, and the pressing danger from the apprehended rescue, and asking the authorization of a military expedition to exterminate the Wyoming people.

Nothing could have been more in consonance with the gubernatorial desire, and orders were immediately issued to Plunkett to raise "the posse," expel the Connecticut men, and "restore peace and good order in the country."

Seven hundred men were raised, and with their munitions and supplies on a large boat, the little army of Pennsylvanians started from

"Fort Augusta" in all the " pomp and circumstance of glorious war," early in December, 1775, bound up the river for the conquest of Yankeedom.

Arrived at the lower end of the valley, and advancing through Nanticoke Gap, the force was confronted by a rude breastwork erected at the point now represented by the inlet lock of the canal on the west side of the river. Here the Connecticut men were securely intrenched, and poured an effective tire upon the invaders. The latter were thrown into the utmost confusion, and hastily crossed the river with their boat. Here they were ambushed, and again routed by another yankee squad. Plunkett threw himself prostrate in the boat to avoid a galling fire, and, ordering a retreat, the whole force retired from the field, leaving it to the victors.

Thus ended the last attempt of Colonial Pennsylvania to possess herself of Wyoming. These desultory warfares were now to be interrupted for a time by a struggle of a more extended and eventful character.

The following year (1776) commenced a new era in the history of the American colonies, A census was taken, and the Westmoreland settlements were found to contain five thousand souls. Their militia amounted to 1100 men capable of bearing arms, and three companies were enlisted at Wyoming for service in the army of the colonies. Regular garrison duty was performed in the several fortifications and a patrol was on duty night and day through the valley.

Early in the spring of 1778 a force of about eight hundred men, composed of British regulars, Tories and Indians, under command of Colonel John Butler, assembled at Niagara and marched for the destruction of Wyoming. The Indians numbered four hundred, and were commanded by Joseph Brant ("Thayendanegea"), a warlike chief of mixed blood.

[The author's statement here is disputed. The late Eleazer Carey has often assured his stepson (C. I. A. C.) that Brant was not at Wyoming, asserting that, while in early youth among the New York Indians, he had frequently heard it claimed, and never denied, that the Indians were led by the chiefs called "Little Beard" and "Blue Throat."]

Embarking on boats and rafts at Tioga Point, the invaders floated down the Susquehanna, landed below the mouth of Bowman's Creek, which enters the river opposite the present flourishing village of

BRANT, THE MOHAWK CHIEF

Tunkhannock, thence marched across the mountains, and entering the Valley, took possession of "Wintermoot's," a fortified settlement occupied by a Tory family and situated about a mile below "Fort Jenkins," a stockade whose site is now covered by the thriving borough of West Pittston. From these headquarters the British commander sent scouting parties throughout the valley. Upon the arrival of the enemy, the settlers collected their principal strength within a fortification situated on the west bank of the river at a large eddy below Monockonock Island. This work had been constructed by forty of the settlers in that vicinity, and thence obtained the name of Forty Fort. The garrison amounted to three hundred and sixty-eight men.

About a month previous, messengers had been sent to the commander-in-chief of the army requesting a detachment for succour. None, however, arrived, and on the morning of the 3rd of July a council was held to determine the question of immediately attacking the enemy or waiting longer for assistance. During this conference five men, citizens of Wyoming, arrived at the fort, three of whom had resigned their commissions in the army. These had heard nothing of the messengers.

The advocates of immediate attack now prevailed in the council, and at dawn of day the little band left the fort and began their march up the valley. Having proceeded about two miles, they halted to reconnoitre, and volunteers were asked for the service. Abraham Pike and an Irish companion (whose name has not been preserved) offered their services. These found the enemy in possession of "Wintermoot's," carousing in supposed security, but on their return the scouts met two strolling Indians, by whom they were fired upon, and immediately returned the fire without effect.

Hastening their advance, the little army found the enemy formed in line of battle—their left under command of Col. John Butler, resting upon the river's bank, and their right, composed of Indians and painted Tories, resting upon the swamp which still appears a prominent feature in the landscape. The settlers immediately deployed and formed in corresponding order—the right commanded by Col. Zebulon Butler and Major John Garrett, the left by Col. Nathan Denison, supported by Lieut. Col. George Dorrance.

It was five o'clock and the battle had begun. It was contested for some time with unflinching courage, each man advancing a few steps at every discharge. The effect was soon apparent upon the British line, which was already slowly retiring, when a horrid yell on the left proclaimed that the savages had penetrated the swamp and turned Denison's wing. He now gave the order to "fall back," intending to double his line at the point menaced and wheel to the left, pivoting upon the centre. This movement was difficult of execution, with raw militia, and the order was misunderstood.

At the same moment the British Colonel Butler succeeded in bringing a party of troops through the bushes on the river's bank and turned the right of the settlers. Thus, enfiladed and outflanked, the latter were forced back on each other, and the rout became general. "Stand up to your work, Sir," said Col. Dorrance to one of his men who was wavering while the Indians were sprinting forward with savage yells.

"Don't leave me, my children!" cried Col. Butler; "stand firm, and the victory is ours!" But all was of no avail; the force of numbers told with fearful effect, and the battle was already lost.

Some of the settlers succeeded in reaching the river, and escaped by swimming; others reached the mountains, after the savages (now occupied by plunder) had given up pursuit. Many of those who escaped, with the women and children, took refuge in Wyoming.

On the next day the combined British and Indian forces appeared there and demanded its surrender. It was stipulated in the articles of capitulation that the garrison was to surrender their prisoners and military stores, and remain in the country unmolested.

Three hundred of the settlers were either killed or missing. Among them were one lieutenant-colonel, one major, ten captains, six lieutenants and two ensigns.

The conditions of the capitulation were entirely disregarded by the victors, and every species of barbarity wantonly committed. No known adjunct of savage cruelty was unemployed upon the defenceless settlement. The village of Wilkes-Barre, then consisting of twenty-three houses, was burned, and men, wives and children separated and borne into captivity. The remaining inhabitants, driven from the valley, wandered on foot sixty miles through the Great Swamp, almost without food or clothing. Numbers perished on the journey, principally women and children, some died of their wounds, while others wandered from the path and were lost.

The Battle and Massacre of Wyoming having produced much public sensation. General Washington sent a detachment of two thousand five hundred men, under command of General John Sullivan, to drive out the British and Indians, restore peace to the valley and lay waste

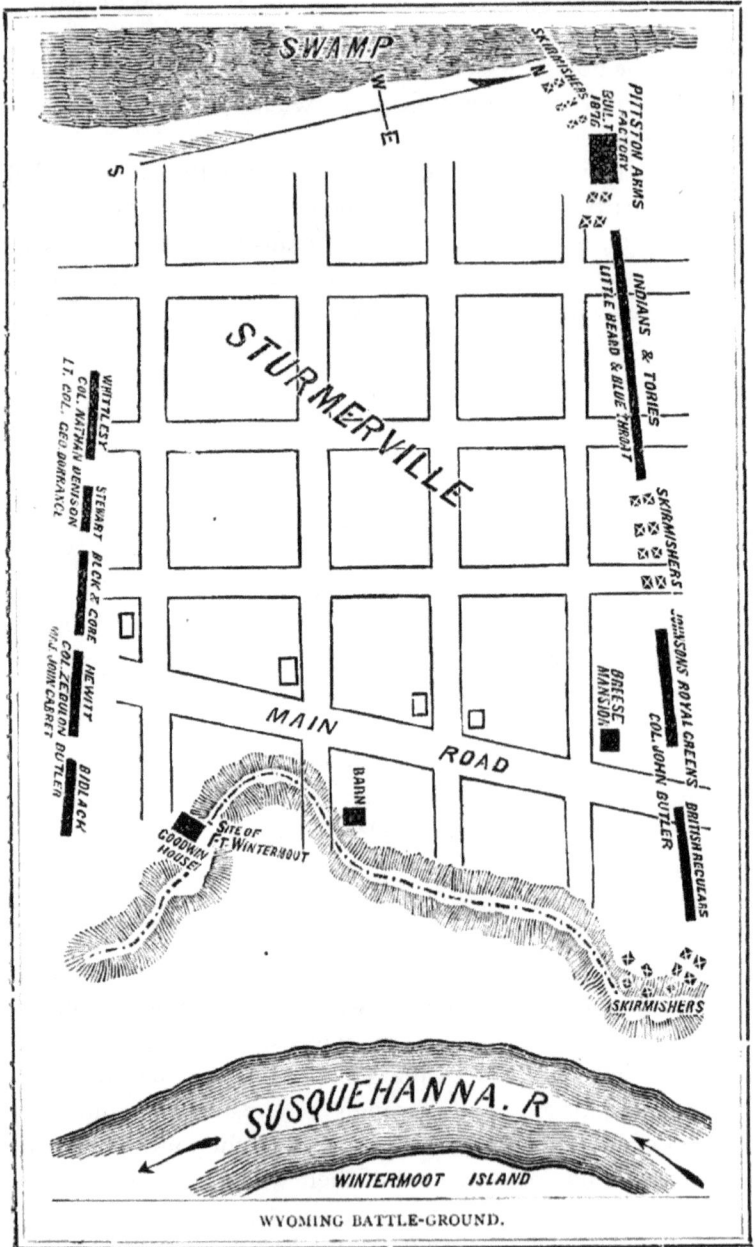

WYOMING BATTLE-GROUND.

the Indian towns of southern New York. This gallant officer arrived with his command on the 22nd of June, 1779, and continued in the valley until the 31st of July. Nine days before, a company of Pennsylvania militia, who had marched to the Lackawaxen, were attacked by one hundred and forty Indians and defeated with the loss of fifty men.

At the same time British and Indian parties attacked Freeland Fort above Northumberland, and Minisink on the Delaware, hoping by these diversions to distract Sullivan from his purpose. No such result occurred. The intrepid officer, putting his whole force in motion, on the last day of July moved from his quarters with pack horses in front, baggage in barges on the river, and martial music front and rear. He camped the first night at Lackawanna, then successively at Buttermilk Falls, Tunkhanrock, Williamson's, Wysauking, Sheshequin and Tioga, and, leaving a garrison at the latter place, pushed on to the attack of the Indian settlements. He found the enemy, in number about a thousand, entrenched behind a breastwork at Newtown (now Elmira), attacked them August 29th. and routed them with considerable slaughter. He then proceeded through the country of the Six Nations, and laid it waste as far as the Genesee River, destroying eighteen villages, with countless orchards and corn-fields. Returning by the same route he was received and entertained with great ceremony by Col. Butler and the settlers who had found their way back.

The danger of Indian incursions now removed, the inhabitants returned in great numbers to Wyoming, where the settlements again flourished and the village was rebuilt.

The state of Pennsylvania, however, viewed with great displeasure a colony within her borders which refused to acknowledge her jurisdiction. She therefore applied to Congress, requesting the appointment of a tribunal to determine the dispute between herself and Connecticut. Congress accordingly appointed a board of commissioners who met at Trenton in December, 1782. Connecticut was represented by Dyer, Johnson and Root; Pennsylvania by Bradford, Reed, Wilson and Sargent. After five weeks of deliberation this body pronounced their opinion as follows:

> We are unanimously of the opinion that the jurisdiction and pre-emption of all land lying within the charter bounds of Pennsylvania, and now claimed by the State of Connecticut, does of right belong to the State of Pennsylvania.

How far *policy*, and not *justice*, affected the rendering of this judgment, has never transpired.

The Connecticut settlers now quietly acquiesced, and united in an humble petition to the General Assembly of Pennsylvania, tendering their allegiance, and asking protection, justice, and a confirmation of their claims. This paper is dated January 18, 1783, and bears the endorsement, "Read January 21st, and ordered to lie on the table."

February 25th, the assembly appointed William Montgomery, Moses McLean and Joseph Montgomery, who were directed "to attend at Wyoming on the 15th of April, act as magistrates, and recommend what measures should be adopted in reference to the Wyoming settlers." These commissioners reported in favour of a reasonable compensation to those fallen in battle against the common enemy, and to those who "should immediately relinquish all claim to the soil and deliver up possession to the rightful owners under Pennsylvania by the first of April next."

Captains Shrawder and Robinson were ordered to march with their companies to Wyoming and occupy the forts and the country. The settlers had understood that the question of political jurisdiction had been settled at Trenton, not the question of private ownership. They now saw before thine eyes another scene opening in which they were to be the passive victims of judicial and executive tyranny, enforced by the bayonets of a commonwealth, which should have welcomed them with open arms and adopted them as her children.

The winter of 1783-4 opened with unexampled severity and continued with uniform cold. In March immense masses of snow and ice went off with sudden thaw and rain. The Susquehanna rose to an unprecedented height, inundating the valley and driving the inhabitants to the hills with the loss of a great portion of their produce and property. The president of the Supreme Executive Council of Pennsylvania, Mr. Dickinson, addressed the General Assembly asking immediate relief for the suffering people of Wyoming.

In the midst of this extreme want, two Justices, Patterson and West, who had accompanied the troops to Wyoming, and to whom the Council had entrusted the administration of affairs, began a system of extortion and tyranny worthy the darkest ages of the world's history. The unhappy husbandman saw his cattle driven off, his barns on fire, and his wife and daughters a prey to a licentious soldiery.

The inhabitants driven to desperation by their calamities, now began to resist their oppressors, and refused to comply with the demands of the mock tribunals established by Patterson and West. Their resistance enraged the magistrates, and on the 12th of May orders were issued to the troops to disarm the people.

Under this pretence, one hundred and fifty families were turned out of their dwellings, many of which were burned, and all ages and sexes reduced to the same dreadful destruction.

Plundered of their remaining property, they were forced out of the valley and driven by the Lackawaxen route to the Delaware country. One shocking instance is mentioned of a mother who actually roasted one of her children piecemeal for the sustenance of the others.

The better feelings of Pennsylvanians, shocked at such barbarities perpetrated upon a defenceless people, now demanded a rigid investigation, in such tones that the General Assembly could not disregard them. Commissioners were sent who examined into the outrages, and made a report, which soon led to the withdrawal of the troops and a proclamation inviting the fugitives to return, under promise of protection.

Many of the troops, however, were still surreptitiously employed by Pennsylvania land claimants. These formed a band of freebooters, who, taking post at Kingston, pillaged the surrounding country. They afterward joined Patterson at Fort Wyoming, which the latter had named "Fort Dickinson." The inhabitants, for their mutual defence and support, garrisoned themselves at Forty Fort.

July 20th, 1784, a party of settlers on their way to the lower flats were ambushed by Patterson's men, and Chester Pierce and Elisha Garrett, two highly respected young men, shot dead. This crowning act of violence aroused a determined spirit of vengeance.

The people, under lead of Col. John Franklin, collected and laid siege to Fort Dickinson, which at that time mounted four pieces of cannon.

While these events were transpiring, the council of Pennsylvania were holding under advisement a new scheme of pacification. John Boyd and John Armstrong were appointed commissioners, with authority "for carrying into execution such measures as shall be judged necessary and expedient for establishing peace and good order in the county of Northumberland." Armstrong and Boyd, with a military force commanded by Col. Moore, marched as far as Pocono Mountain, where they were met by a party of settlers, commanded by Captain John Swift. Desultory firing occurred, killing one of the Pennsylvania party and wounding two others, after which the Connecticut

Jn. Sullivan

men withdrew.

Armstrong entered the valley with a small force, and was joined by Magistrates Hewitt, Mead and Martin, with a party of men from Northumberland. These together constituted a force of about 400 men under Col. Armstrong. This celebrated functionary, who subsequently filled the position of Secretary of War and Minister to France, had little stomach for an open conflict with the settlers. Through life it was his preference to obtain his objects by stratagem and duplicity. Declaring by proclamation that he had come only to protect the defenceless and enforce peace, he wheedled the settlers into a conference, took them prisoners, and despatched forty, bound with ropes, to Sunbury, and the balance, tied in pairs, to Easton. Most of the troops were now discharged, leaving however a sufficient garrison in Fort Dickinson, while Armstrong, Patterson and their associates proceeded to gather the harvest and appropriate it to their own use.

Many settlers residing remote from the scene of these events now commenced coming in, and appointed a rendezvous at Bowman's Creek. So soon as the party considered themselves strong enough, they set out for the valley, reoccupied Forty Fort, and commenced operations against Armstrong. The latter, after several skirmishes and the capture of a part of the arms and ammunition of the settlers, concluded to repair to Philadelphia to report progress and demand reinforcements.

Sept. 27th, fifteen of the people surrounded the house of Patterson and his commissioners, and commenced an assault, which lasted two hours, resulting in the death of Reed and Henderson, two of the Pennsylvania magistrates. The council at Philadelphia, hearing of these events, after consultation with Armstrong, ordered that fifty men of the militia of Bucks County, and a like number from Berks County, be equipped and despatched to Wyoming, "for quieting the disturbances and supporting the civil authority in that district," appointing at the same time John Armstrong to be Adjutant General.

This enterprise was opposed by John Dickinson, Esq., president of the council, who set forth his views in a letter still on file; whereupon the council resolved "that the measures adopted on the 2nd inst. be pursued," and on the same day issued a proclamation offering a reward of twenty-five pounds sterling for the apprehension of fifteen of the principal inhabitants of Wyoming. Armstrong met with no little difficulty in organizing the second expedition. The opinion was gaining ground that the Connecticut settlers at Wyoming were a persecuted people. He, however, commenced his march with only forty men, and arrived in the Valley on the 16th of October, the settlers retiring into garrison at Forty Fort.

The "Council of Censors" (an institution erected by the first Constitution of Pennsylvania, and clothed with the general power of revising all legislation, examining the disposition of taxes, and generally guarding the popular interest) had made special call for persons and papers touching the difficulties at Wyoming. This call was contemptuously refused by the General Assembly, but the refusal only confirmed the censors in their opinion "of the truth of the complaints from Wyoming, and the utter neglect of the Government to protect the oppressed inhabitants." They say:

> And lastly, we regret the fatal example these proceedings have set—of private persons, at least equally able with their opponents to maintain their own cause, procuring the interest of the commonwealth and the aid of the public treasury in their behalf. We therefore hold this business up to public censure, to prevent, if possible, further instances of bad government which might convulse and disturb our new formed nation.

Notwithstanding this remonstrance from so high a source, the Supreme Executive Council, in contempt of public opinion, proceeded to exert their utmost endeavours to furnish Armstrong with re-enforcements. In this they failed, and the redoubtable leader was compelled to remain with his forty men in the ruins of Fort Dickinson, too weak for extended plunder or even for a successful attack upon his enemies at Forty Fort. These latter held stubbornly to their post while they gathered in the remnant of their crops, meantime joining ia petitions to the legislatures both of Pennsylvania and Connecticut.

As winter approached, Armstrong abandoned the block house, disbanded his troops, and returned to Philadelphia. Thus ended the last expedition fitted out by Pennsylvania to persecute and destroy her own peaceful citizens.

March, 1787, the people of Wyoming, hopeless of any equitable settlement of their claims, now offered a compromise, proposing to the General Assembly that if the Commonwealth would grant them the seventeen townships which had been laid out and settled previous to the Decree of Trenton, they would relinquish all claims to other lands on the Susquehanna purchase. In consideration of this agreement being confirmed by the Assembly, the Pennsylvania claimants

TIMOTHY PICKERING

were to relinquish such lands (lying within the same townships) as the State had previously granted them.

Accordingly (28th of March, 1787), a law was passed, complying with the request of the inhabitants, and under it commissioners were appointed to *re-survey* the lots claimed by the settlers, and give them *certificates* of the regularity of their claims. Hence our term, "*Certified Townships.*" These commissioners—Timothy Pickering, William Montgomery and Stephen Balliot, shortly proceeded to Wyoming and entered upon their duties. The abduction of Pickering and his subsequent rescue were startling episodes to vary the scene, but of small historic importance. There was, however, a class of persons of a different character from those concerned in this lawless outrage, to whom the State had sold lands. These viewed with intense disgust an act of the Legislature to deprive them of their lands in favour of the Connecticut claimants.

Opposition from these was seated and strenuous, leading to the repeal of the law—again opening the question, and subjecting the country to all the evils of uncertain land tenure. Wisdom and justice, however finally prevailed over factious selfishness and greed Pennsylvania had adopted a new Constitution and was now governed by a more liberal policy. Petitions poured in for the enactment of some measure to make final disposition of the long-vexed question; and in April, 1789, an act was passed for a final settlement of the controversy so far as related to the "Seventeen Townships."

By this act, commissioners were appointed, to cause a survey of all lands claimed by the Connecticut settlers, and which had been assigned them previous to the Decree of Trenton, to value the lands, to divide them into four classes of lots, according to quality, to make out a "Certificate" for each claimant, specifying the number, location and quality of his acres with attached draft. Also to re-survey all the lands claimed by Pennsylvania claimants within the seventeen townships, which should be released or reconveyed to the Commonwealth, and divide the same into four classes, according to their value. As soon as forty thousand acres should be released to the state, and the Connecticut settlers claiming to the same amount should bind themselves to submit to the determination of the commissioners, the law was to take effect.

The Pennsylvania claimants were to be *compensated* from the State Treasury at the rate of *five dollars* per acre for lands of the first class, *three dollars* per acre tor lands of the second class, *fifty cents* per acre for lands of the third class, and *twenty-five cents* for lands of the fourth class. The Connecticut claimants were to receive patents from the State confirming their lands, on condition of paying *two dollars* per acre for the first class, *one dollar and twenty cents* for the second class, *fifty cents* for the third class, and *eight and one third cents* for the fourth class. Thus, while the state was selling her wild lands to her other citizens at twenty cents per acre, she demanded of the Connecticut settlers a sum which, upon the supposition that there was the same quantity of land in each class, would average ninety-four cents. This law, however, terminated the long and bloody controversy known as the "Pennamite War," which covering the seven years of the Revolution, had continued from 1762 to 1787.

These old claims having thus been adjusted, and the Pennsylvania Title fully established, Luzerne county erected in 1787, and Bradford and Susquehanna counties in their turn—the famous "Wyoming Controversy" became a memory of the past, and the "beautiful valley," under a mild and liberal government, enjoyed that repose which a long term of unparalleled sufferings rendered necessary to its happiness and prosperity.

www.ingramcontent.com/pod-product-compliance
Lightning Source LLC
Chambersburg PA
CBHW021108090426
42738CB00006B/557